BRITAIN'S BEST POLITICAL CARTOONS 2017

Dr Tim Benson is Britain's leading authority on political cartoons. He runs The Political Cartoon Gallery and Café which is located near the River Thames in Putney. He has produced numerous books on the history of cartoons, including *Giles's War*, *Churchill in Caricature*, *Low and the Dictators*, *The Cartoon Century: Modern Britain through the Eyes of Its Cartoonists*, *Drawing the Curtain: The Cold War in Cartoons* and *Over the Top: A Cartoon History of Australia at War.*

BRITAIN'S BEST POLITICAL CARTOONS 2017

Edited by Tim Benson

rh
BOOKS

1 3 5 7 9 10 8 6 4 2

Random House Books
20 Vauxhall Bridge Road
London SW1V 2SA

Random House Books is part of the Penguin Random House
group of companies whose addresses can be found
at global.penguinrandomhouse.com

Penguin
Random House
UK

First published by Random House Books in 2017

www.penguin.co.uk

A CIP catalogue record for this book is available from the British Library

ISBN 9781847948076

Typeset in 11/15.5 pt Amasis MT Light by Jouve (UK), Milton Keynes

Printed and bound in Italy by LEGO, S.p.A.

Penguin Random House is committed to a sustainable future
for our business, our readers and our planet. This book is made from
Forest Stewardship Council® certified paper.

INTRODUCTION

Theresa May. Nicola Sturgeon. Angela Merkel. The last few years have witnessed an extraordinary increase in the number of women in British politics. It's a refreshing change from the overwhelming blokeyness that has defined our political culture for centuries. But it also presents a new challenge for the UK's political cartoonists, who have become used to drawing white men in dark suits. For artists from *The Times*'s Peter Brookes to the *Guardian*'s Nicola Jennings, the rise of women in politics has transformed the nature of political satire.

That's not to say that women have only recently started to crop up in political cartoons. Although Parliament has always been male dominated, since the nineteenth century female characters have been used to symbolise the nation state, most famously in the work of Sir Bernard Partridge and Sir John Tenniel: take such instantly recognisable figures as Britannia, the symbol of Britain, Marianne for the French Republic, Germania for Germany or the Statue of Liberty for the United States. Even Mother Russia has sometimes been called upon for tragic events, as she comes across as a more sympathetic figure than the Russian Bear. In the 1920s, David Low sought to revitalise Britain's national symbols by inventing Joan Bull – a 'flapper', complete with a bob and a trendy skirt – as a topical reinvention of John Bull and Britannia. Unlike Low's creation Colonel Blimp, however, Joan Bull was considered rather bland and failed to capture the public's imagination. Today, many cartoonists consider all national symbols somewhat passé,

David Low's updated version of John Bull, the 'flapper' Joan Bull.

although Britannia still occasionally crops up in the cartoon pages of Britain's broadsheets.

Since 1953, and the accession of Elizabeth II to the throne, cartoonists have become used to drawing a female head of state. At first, satirists treated her with extreme deference: since readers were more than likely to protest if her face was depicted in cartoon form, artists felt it necessary to show her only from behind. But by the late 1960s, as society gradually became less submissive, cartoonists started to feel more confident about satirising her. Even today, however, she tends to get off quite lightly by comparison with others (in part because she stands above the political affray). Though that's not to say that she is never a target – in 2016, for example, Steve Bell drew a cartoon that showed her naked bottom. The *Guardian*, deeming this to be in poor taste, cropped the image.

The rise of Margaret Thatcher made women more prominent in traditional, party-political satire. Female politicians were still a comparative rarity at the time, and there was some uncertainty as to how much vitriol was permissible. 'As the first female prime minister [Thatcher] caused problems for cartoonists who were all men,' recalls Steve Bell. 'She definitely benefitted from a kind of misplaced deference that men feel they owe women and many male cartoonists' depictions of that sex were less

The Queen is still treated with some deference by newspaper editors: this cartoon by Steve Bell was cropped by the *Guardian*'s editors to omit the royal bottom.

than subtle at the best of times, veering between waspie-waisted, big-boobed stereotyping and excessive reverence.' In his view, satirists developed a rather patronising way of depicting Thatcher: they gave her 'male' characteristics. 'She was portrayed, particularly in *Spitting Image*, as a woman with balls, which was shocking, not for its devastating political penetration, but for its blundering misogyny,' says Bell. For those who did not go down that route, such as the *Daily Mail*'s 'Mac', it was a question of picking on the physical characteristics that marked her apart – her distinctive handbag and hairdo. Mac actually preferred drawing Margaret's husband Dennis – until the real Dennis Thatcher staggered up to him at a cocktail party and called him a 'bastard' for always portraying him drunk. It was only later in Mrs Thatcher's career that Steve Bell, for one, took a different approach. 'There was an innate madness about her that my colleagues just didn't get,' he says. Accordingly, he started to draw her with bulging eyes and a vacant, sinister smile.

Today, the increasing number of female MPs is regarded as a positive boon by some cartoonists. In their view, male politicians are becoming ever more indistinguishable – whereas women offer a chance for artists to be more creative. According to the *Telegraph*'s Bob Moran, 'In some ways, female politicians are easier for cartoonists. Unlike their male counterparts, women politicians do not all wear the same suits, shoes and hairstyles. So there is more to differentiate them beyond just their faces.' Morten Morland of *The Times* agrees: 'Female politicians can be more interesting – even easier to draw – because of their wardrobe, for example. Not always in black or blue suits, they often have more elements to work with than just facial features.' Or, as Scott Clissold of the *Sunday Express* and the *Star* puts it, 'I'm sick of drawing grey old farts in dark suits so the more women in politics the better.'

Indeed, one gets the impression that some female politicians have capitalised on cartoonists' love of distinctive, instantly recognisable characteristics. Take Margaret Thatcher's famous handbag, which rapidly became cartoonists' visual shorthand for her power and femininity. Thatcher also cultivated a distinctively regal haircut, which cartoonists frequently picked up on: according to Nicola Jennings, Thatcher 'ended up trying to emulate the Queen. Her hair was a visual hook.' Across the Pond,

The Not-So-Iron Lady: Theresa May by Morten Morland for the *Spectator*.

during the US presidential election in 2016, Hillary Clinton became renowned for her brightly coloured suits, which soon became a staple of cartoons in the American press – to the extent that her supporters branded themselves the 'pantsuit nation'. And here in the UK, Theresa May has tried to do something similar with her distinctive footwear. Steve Bell has made a point of drawing oversized leopard-print heels into every depiction of the prime minister, and May herself has become known for wearing them at every major speech; Bell even once saw her showing off her shoes to the photographers at a party conference.

There is a difficult balance to be achieved here. Focus too much on things like fashion accessories, and it can lead to accusations of sexism. Make your caricatures too harsh and 'male' and the same problem arises: the veteran cartoonist Andy Davey, for example, has found that his drawings of women have a tendency to become more masculine with every line he adds. Yet if you pull your punches too much then the same criticism can be made. As Peter Brookes points out, 'A big challenge is not to hold back out of a sense of, for want of a better word, chivalry. Thank God Theresa May is so politically awful that the thought doesn't enter your head!' Bob Moran neatly summarises the dilemma every cartoonist faces:

There is an idea that a cartoonist should be 'kinder' to a female politician, suggesting that women are more easily offended when somebody mocks their appearance. This line of thought is, of course, sexist. However, if a cartoonist were to apply exactly the same approach to a woman as they would a man, exaggerating or underlining certain physical attributes like the size of their nose, breasts or bottom, they are just as likely to be accused of sexism. Walking that tightrope is perhaps the biggest challenge presented by female politicians.

Scott Clissold makes a similar point. He has noticed 'a very fine line where overdoing the cruelty/crudity with a female politician has the danger of creating the opposite effect of what was intended.' And, of course, 'The last thing you want is the reader feeling sympathy for the politician and missing the point of the cartoon.' The *London Evening Standard*'s Christian Adams has experienced this first-hand, receiving criticism from angry readers for drawing Theresa May with a 'wonky nose' (the Prime Minister herself has said she hates the shape of her nose). It is, needless to say, an objection he never heard when drawing men's faces.

Although Britain's mostly left-leaning cartoonists are disappointed that Theresa May struggles on as prime minister, she at least offers them plenty of material for their daily output. 'With May you can draw her unsteady, panicky, not quite

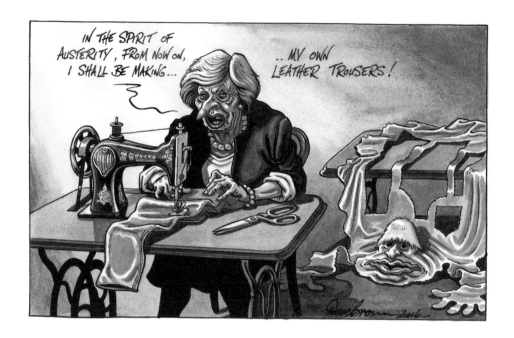

IN THE SPIRIT OF AUSTERITY, FROM NOW ON, I SHALL BE MAKING...

.. MY OWN LEATHER TROUSERS!

Cartoonists such as Dave Brown have often focused on Theresa May's distinctive fashion sense – especially her famous leather trousers.

sure of herself as she's still finding her feet,' says Scott Clissold. 'She has these great long legs so it's like watching a giraffe learn to ski.' According to Steve Bell, May is a 'very striking woman who visually puts herself out there, which luckily doesn't always work out for her. Her demeanour can be awkward which can be visually disturbing at times.' During the 2016 global 'scary clown' craze, in which people disguised themselves as clowns to scare strangers, Bell began to portray May in face paint and a clown wig. 'Why a clown?' Bell asks. 'I don't know. Maybe it was those pantaloony trousers

she occasionally wears. She does have a white pale face and her stark eyes and mouth stand out clearly.' Elsewhere, cartoonists have had great fun with the comparison May made between her leadership and that of Queen Elizabeth I – something that Morten Morland, Martin Rowson and Brian Adcock all duly capitalised on.

Compared with Margaret Thatcher, Theresa May has had a very rough ride in political satire. This might just be a sign of the times – cartoonists are arguably becoming more acerbic by the year. But according to Peter Brookes, May has brought her harsh treatment on herself. Thatcher and May, he says, are 'like chalk and cheese . . . Whether you agreed with them or not, Thatcher, like Corbyn, held strong beliefs. Does May believe in anything? Search me.' The freelance cartoonist David Simonds agrees: Thatcher was a 'conviction politician', who was rarely portrayed as 'showing any hint of doubt carrying out her policies. Thatcher was portrayed as the Iron Lady who was an implacable force, whereas the portrayals of Theresa May up to now have shown her greatly weakened by the election result while struggling with the Herculean problems of Brexit,' he says. 'She did try to reinvent herself as "Maggie Version 2.0" by calling a snap general election in June 2017 – and we all know how that turned out!'

It must be admitted that the rise of female politicians has not been matched by the rise of female political cartoonists. From the great pioneers of cartooning like James Gillray, John Tenniel and David Low, right through to modern-day masters like Steve Bell and Peter Brookes, all the most famous figures in cartoon history have been men. Of course, Fleet Street itself was male-dominated for a long time. Colin Seymour-Ure, who has written widely about the British press, recalls that when his journalist father left the Reporters' Room at *The Times* in about 1970, 'they had never had a female reporter since my father joined in 1928'. The first female political correspondent, the *Observer*'s Leah Beloff, was not appointed until 1964, and it was not until the late 1980s that female editors began to be appointed for the first time. Today, though, the world of journalism has opened up – whereas the doors of the political cartoon world have remained resolutely closed to women. In fact, the UK has never had a full-time female political cartoonist on any national newspaper.

There is an extent to which this reflects women's marginalisation in the art world more broadly. Even though it would appear that many of the earliest artists may well have been female – recent research has discovered that cavemen's hand paintings, arguably the first cartoons, were almost certainly drawn by women – they have been largely excluded ever since, particularly by the inhabitants of the macho world of political journalism.

That's not to say that there have been no female cartoonists, or women who have drawn political satires. There have, and many have been highly talented – they have just tended to be side-lined. The first female political cartoonist, whose works were published in the 1910s, was Ruby Lindsay, sister of the great Australian cartoonist Norman Lindsay, and wife of the radical *Daily Herald* cartoonist Will Dyson. Because her drawing style was almost identical to her husband's, she sometimes helped him complete his cartoons. And while her ambitions lay primarily with painting, she regularly produced discretely initialled political cartoons that were published in Christabel Pankhurst's magazine, *The Suffragette*. She also drew artwork for posters supporting socialist causes. Tragically, she fell victim to the Spanish Flu epidemic that swept through Europe at the end of the First World War and died in 1919, only a year after women finally gained the right to vote.

Just under 20 years later, the cartoons of another Australian woman, Antonia Yeoman, started appearing in *Punch* magazine. Yeoman was strictly a gag cartoonist (she once told an interviewer that she was not interested in politics), but even though she avoided controversial contemporary issues she still felt it necessary to work under a male pseudonym – 'Anton'. When readers of the magazine discovered her gender, a number were less than impressed. She later recalled that 'a couple of bishops had given up *Punch* when I started drawing for them'.

After the Second World War, the number of female cartoonists contributing to Britain's magazines gradually increased. In the early 1950s, a cartoon

JUSTICE—ANOTHER WRONGED WOMAN.

One of Ruby Lindsay's cartoons for *The Suffragette*. In the original, the man is accusing Justice of supporting women's suffrage: 'Enough of that . . . I've suspected all along you were on their side!'

strip in the *Evening Standard* entitled 'Mandy, Mops and Cubby', produced by Dorothy M. Wheeler and Enid Blyton, became the first cartoon strip in a major newspaper to be created by an all-female team. The

Daily Express, too, began to include women's cartoons. 'The Gambols', a light-hearted strip that was first published in 1950, was usually credited to Barry Appleby – but today, experts think that his wife, Doris 'Dobs' Appleby, wrote most of the jokes. And in 1951, Margaret Belsky began drawing pocket cartoons for the *Daily Herald*. Her style was not overtly political – she preferred gag cartoons, similar to the *Daily Telegraph*'s 'Matt' today. Belsky was the first woman to draw a daily front-page cartoon for a national newspaper, but the paper did not reveal this to its readers, who knew nothing about their cartoonist behind the signature, 'Belsky'. She modestly referred to herself as 'just a hack' and 'a poor man's Osbert Lancaster' – quite the understatement, considering her unique place in cartoon history.

Yet through this period, women continued to be excluded from traditional political cartooning. Just how unfriendly the environment was is illustrated by an incident at *Punch* in March 1972. The magazine decided that it should acknowledge the rise of the feminist movement in Britain by producing its first ever women's issue – to feature an all-female cast of writers, editors and cartoonists. The gag cartoonist Sally Artz was given the honour of producing a full-colour cartoon for the cover. But at the last moment, fearing a backlash from *Punch*'s

"You haven't been flossing, have you?"

One of Martha Richler's 'light' cartoons for the *Evening Standard*, published when Saddam Hussein was captured after months in hiding.

middle-aged male audience, her cartoon was relegated to an inside page and long-time *Punch* contributor Michael Ffolkes was enlisted to draw the cover instead. To rub salt into the wound, Ffolkes drew a misogynistic cartoon. Artz recalls that it was 'more Donald McGill than *Punch*, with a huge, bosomy woman (accompanied by tiny hen-pecked husband) being shown the wine label, in a restaurant by the leering wine waiter. We were all pretty pissed off by the whole MCP [male chauvinist pig] attitude.' Most journalists were frightened by the feminist movement at the time. *Punch* cartoonist John Jensen tried to sell his own *Women in*

Caricature book project in the 1970s and was 'greeted with slack jaws and total incomprehension by the all-male publishers, all dead-scared – then – of feminism'.

Arguably the atmosphere had not changed that much some four decades later, when another female cartoonist began work in Fleet Street. In 2003, Martha Richler – who, under the gender-neutral pseudonym 'Marf', had drawn a pocket cartoon for the *Evening Standard*'s Letters page since 2001 – became its main cartoonist. Richler soon sensed hostility from some in Fleet Street. 'I felt extra pressure to prove myself as they assumed I was less intelligent and less capable because I was female,' she recalls. She also felt that she was under some pressure not to come up with work that was too probing: 'I wanted to do both darker subjects and lighter ones. I often presented much darker and more political ideas to the editor. It was a source of great frustration to me that I wasn't given the freedom to switch between darker themes and lighter ones.' Richler's material did not go down well with her colleagues, who, she says, 'did not like the feminine character of [her] work'. After only a year, the decision was taken to replace the newspaper's political cartoon – which had been there since 1927 – with a celebrity photograph. Today, the only daily newspaper that draws on the work of (unpaid) female political cartoonists is the left-wing *Morning Star*, which has a tiny circulation of 10,000. It is another troubling reminder that, when it comes to political cartoons, Fleet Street remains a man's world.

Today, there are numerous female political cartoonists working for major newspapers, from Cathy Wilcox in Australia to Sharon Murdoch in New Zealand to Ann Telnaes in the United States. Even Saudi Arabia has one or two. But while Britain has no shortage of hilarious female cartoonists, traditional political cartooning has remained something of a closed shop. The issue has not gone unnoticed: the *Guardian*'s Posy Simmonds – easily Britain's most famous female cartoonist – says she has been asked about cartooning's lack of women dozens of times.

Various theories have been floated as to why this should be. One is that female cartoonists are excluded by the testosterone-fuelled atmosphere of the world of political cartoons. Ella Bucknall, founder of the all-female political cartoon zine *Whip*, said recently, 'As it stands, the world of political cartooning is just one all-boys club scoffing at another all-boys club.' Women, it seems, have been cut out of this circle. Nicola Jennings makes a similar point: in a world where most cartoonists are male, women end up being held to a much higher standard. 'Some men . . . cannot cope with being lampooned by a woman,' she says. 'If you are not that good as a cartoonist, you will not get away with it as a woman.'

This masculine atmosphere extends to the social side of cartooning, too. 'I'm very fond of many of my colleagues and enjoy their company,' says the freelancer Peter Schrank, 'but I'm always aware of a strong sense of hierarchy; there's a lot of male competition and jostling for position. It's quite a macho scene.' For their part, the *Guardian*'s Nicola Jennings and the former strip cartoonist Maggie Ling both point to a male 'clubby culture' in newsrooms and among cartoonists, whose social lives have a tendency to centre on pubs and drinking. 'They are invariably boozy, blokey affairs,' says the veteran cartoonist Rick Brookes, 'and women attending such events are not only unimpressed but feel quite left out.'

Another suggestion is that male editors still feel uneasy about cartooning styles they feel to be 'feminine'. 'Given a hypothetical choice between a male and a female cartoonist of equal drawing ability, [editors] would believe the male to be more ruthless, and therefore make the better political satirist,' suggests the *Sun*'s Steve Bright. 'I have to say that this does not necessarily tie in with my general life's experiences . . . but there are some paths I hesitate to tread.' Morten Morland agrees

that this bias plays a role. He attributes the gender imbalance to 'the style of drawing which has become associated with cartoons' – a style that has historically been considered 'masculine' and aggressive. 'I don't think editors are brave enough in trying alternative styles,' Morland says. 'Cartoonists like [the *Washington Post*'s] Ann Telnaes prove that a more stylised/feminine line can be just as biting as the angrier ink splat approach.'

All this raises the shadow of a final possible explanation. Perhaps it is that many women cartoonists simply dislike the traditional language of political drawings – they feel the ground rules have been set by men, and this is a chauvinistic world they simply don't want to join. Putting it at its most simple, political cartooning involves reducing important and complex political debates to jibes about bickering politicians. It might simply be something that women cartoonists don't want to be a part of. 'I don't want to spend my day drawing liars and crooks,' says Nicola Jennings. 'My male counterparts seem to know it's all a game. I'm interested in exposing the truth, but I prefer to do it through caricature.' Maggie Ling agrees. A lot of political cartoons obsess over petty power struggles – a theme that, in her view, interests men much more than women. Perhaps, then, political

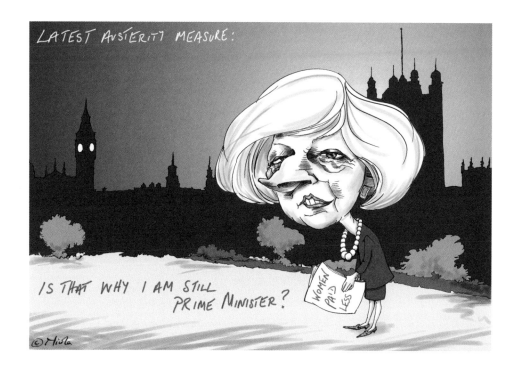

LATEST AUSTERITY MEASURE:

IS THAT WHY I AM STILL PRIME MINISTER?

WOMEN PAID LESS

©Niola

Nicola Jennings's caricature of Theresa May, published in the *Guardian* during the scandal over female BBC presenters being paid less than men.

cartooning is one glass ceiling that talented female cartoonists have decided is not really worth cracking.

Except that political cartooning is always evolving. And, of course, there are a lot of extraordinarily talented women satirists around, whether gag writers, strip or social commentary cartoonists, authors of graphic novels or stand-up comics. The internet has allowed female political cartoonists to reach new audiences: as the

US-based cartoonist Liza Donnelly has commented, 'Social media is allowing women's art to be seen even from places like Iran and China.' And the traditional home of political cartoons – the broadsheet press – is changing too. As of 2017, there are only six full-time political cartoonists at work in Britain: Steve Bell, Peter Brookes, Christian Adams, Dave Brown, Patrick Blower and 'Mac'. Another dozen cartoonists fill in when these six are away, or are employed to do one or two cartoons a week. Perhaps, as this generation approaches retirement, there will be women as well as men to take their place: as Scott Clissold puts it, the world of comics and illustration is already 'packed full of female artists and creators as there are more opportunities and more work about'. Clissold suggests that most newspapers today are more than open to the prospect of employing a female cartoonist: 'Peter Brookes on *The Times* and Steve Bell on the *Guardian* are brilliant political cartoonists, who happen to be men. Newspapers are pretty cutthroat. If there were better political cartoonists, female or male, knocking on the door with better political cartoons (good luck finding any!), I'm pretty certain they'd be given a chance.'

'Perhaps there should be an enquiry to investigate this issue,' former *Sun* cartoonist Dave Gaskill quips. 'Headed by either Leveson or Chilcot.' But he adds a warning: in an era of declining newspaper sales, the slots open to promising new talent are limited. It is a problem that Britain's female cartoonists are only too aware of. 'Maybe, in the future, there will be a female Peter Brookes,' says Sally Artz. 'She had better hurry up, before the last newspaper goes online!'

THE CARTOONS

The Beautiful Wall

2 September 2016
Martin Rowson
Guardian

Donald Trump insisted that Mexico would pay for an 'impenetrable and beautiful' wall along America's southern border. The Republican presidential nominee told a rally of his supporters that Mexicans 'don't know it yet but they are going to pay for the wall'. Trump also said that, if elected president, he would deport 11 million illegal immigrants from the US.

Strikes at Southern Rail, complaints from NHS junior doctors and concerns over Chinese plans to build a power station in Britain all caused growing criticism of Theresa May. The former Tory chancellor Ken Clarke accused her of running 'a government with no policies', claiming that 'nobody' had a plan to get Britain out of the EU.

4 September 2016
Chris Riddell
Observer

7 September 2016
Peter Brookes
The Times

Keith Vaz, Labour MP for Leicester East, stepped down as chairman of the Home Affairs Select Committee following claims that he had paid for the services of two male sex workers. The *Sunday Mirror* had published a recording of Vaz meeting up with two escorts and discussing sex and drugs, telling them 'we need to get this party started'.

Justine Greening, the education secretary, outlined proposals that would allow the foundation of new grammar schools. After Labour condemned the move, Greening said that selective grammar schools could play an important role in education, but that the government wanted them to be 'inclusive' and that she did not want a 'return to the past'.

9 September 2016
Steve Bell
Guardian

9 September 2016
Christian Adams
Daily Telegraph

Republican presidential candidate Donald Trump praised Vladimir Putin for his 'very strong control' of Russia, saying 'he's been a leader . . . far more than our president has been a leader'. Trump also mentioned that he was pleased to have received a compliment from the Russian president. According to the cartoonist, Putin enjoys being portrayed as menacing and sinister – even playing up to it for the cameras – so being depicted as a Bond villain was probably right up his street.

A few days previously, North Korean leader Kim Jong-un had declared that his government would continue to develop nuclear weapons. 'I'm always happy when I'm able to produce an image that's as simple as possible – when a news story lends itself to something bold – as I think they're the easiest to digest,' says the cartoonist. 'Kim Jong-un, like Trump, is a gift to cartoonists due to his incredible hair, among other things. Unfortunately though, a gift to cartoonists isn't always a good thing for the world in general.'

10 September 2016
Ben Jennings
Guardian

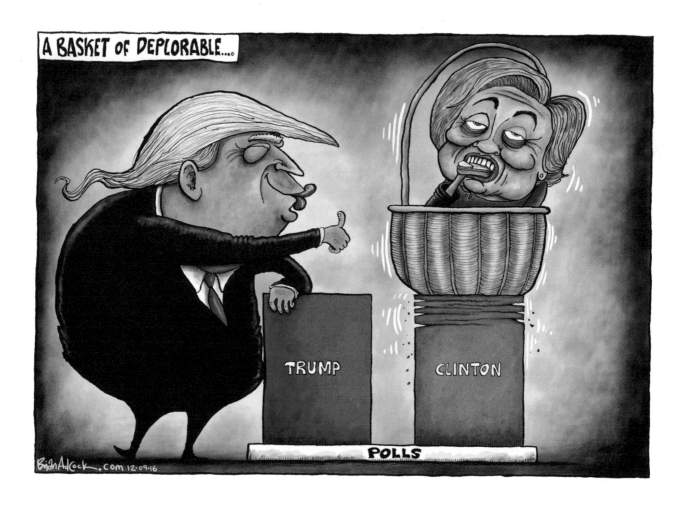

A BASKET OF DEPLORABLE....

TRUMP

CLINTON

POLLS

Brian Adcock .com 12·09·16

12 September 2016
Brian Adcock
Independent

According to the cartoonist, 'During the presidential election campaign Hillary Clinton suffered a drop in the polls following a bizarre comment calling the supporters of Trump "a basket of deplorables". I remember being shocked by her saying this when I saw it on TV, and trying to work out what possible benefit there was to insulting a massive swathe of the electorate. No benefit at all, as it turned out.'

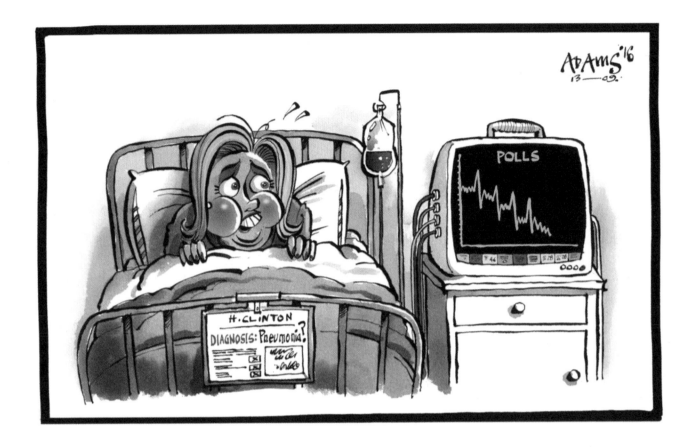

The Democrats' presidential nominee Hillary Clinton collapsed at an event commemorating the September 11 attacks. Videos circulated that showed the 68-year-old being hauled into a black van by her aides, with her feet dragging along beneath her. At first, Clinton's campaign staff said that she had just 'overheated' at the ceremony; but later it was revealed that the former first lady was suffering from pneumonia, and that her strategists had known this all along. The development came just as Trump was catching up with Clinton in the polls, and further contributed to the perception that she was dishonest.

13 September 2016
Christian Adams
Daily Telegraph

The production company behind *The Great British Bake Off* caused controversy by moving the show from the BBC to Channel 4. In the same week, former prime minister David Cameron announced that he was resigning as an MP. Cameron had previously said that he wanted to stay in Parliament until at least 2020, leading commentators to speculate that there had been a rift between him and Theresa May, and that he was quitting to find a more financially lucrative job.

14 September 2016
Peter Brookes
The Times

A parliamentary report concluded that David Cameron's 'ill-conceived' military intervention in Libya in 2011 had contributed to the rise of Islamic State. It said that his decision to help topple Muammar Gaddafi had been based on a series 'erroneous assumptions'. In March, Barack Obama had criticised Cameron for becoming 'distracted' after the intervention, and allowing the country to become a 'shit show'.

15 September 2016
Steve Bell
Guardian

BIG SHOES TO FILL...

17 September 2016
Ben Jennings
i

This cartoon was published when Diane James was in charge of UKIP, following Nigel Farage's decision to step down. 'When the UKIP brand is so synonymous with one man, no one can quite fill the shoes,' says the cartoonist. 'Paul Nuttall hung up his football boots to give it a go after Diane James, but was still not up to it.'

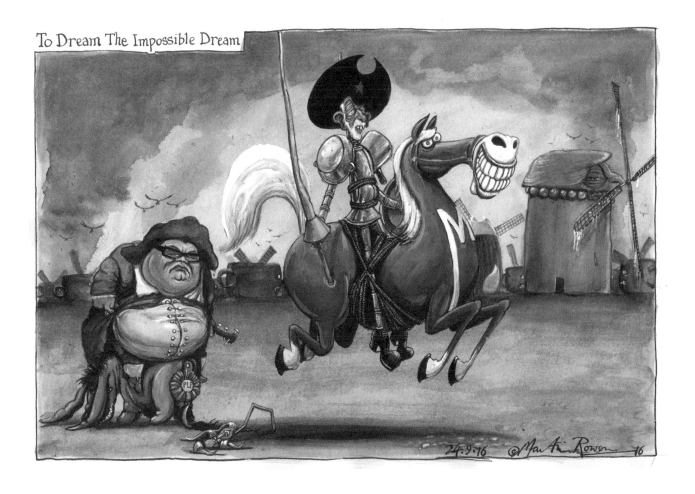

To Dream The Impossible Dream

Jeremy Corbyn promised to 'wipe the slate clean' after defeating Owen Smith in the bitterly fought Labour leadership contest. Corbyn called for an end to party infighting, saying that he had secured his second mandate in a year. This cartoon refers to the song 'The Impossible Dream' from the 1972 film *Man of La Mancha*, which featured Peter O'Toole as the charismatic and idealistic knight Don Quixote.

24 September 2016
Martin Rowson
Guardian

27 September 2016
Morten Morland
The Times

At the Labour Party conference in Liverpool, Shadow Chancellor John McDonnell was ridiculed after he referenced John Lennon's song 'Imagine' in his speech. 'In the birthplace of John Lennon, it falls to us to inspire people to imagine,' he said. 'Imagine the society that we can create. It's a society that's radically transformed, radically fairer, more equal and more democratic.'

Hillary Clinton and Donald Trump clashed at the first of the three US presidential debates. Clinton was widely thought to have won the debate, offering detailed policy suggestions on issues ranging from taxes to foreign policy. Trump, on the other hand, was criticised for interrupting Clinton, and for seeming erratic, irritable and rude: at one point, he told the Democratic nominee that she didn't 'have the stamina' to be president.

27 September 2016
KAL
Economist

A think tank released a report that concluded that 'political squabbles and turf wars' were undermining the government's Brexit plan. It criticised Theresa May's decision to divide power between three different Brexit ministers, Liam Fox, David Davis and Boris Johnson – the so-called 'three Brexiteers'. The Institute for Government's report, *Planning for Brexit: Silence Is Not a Strategy*, said the 'triple departmental structure risks creating fragmentation and incoherence, and a lack of clarity about the roles and responsibilities of the new departments'.

30 September 2016
Dave Brown
Independent

In his first speech as chancellor of the exchequer, Philip Hammond signalled a departure from his predecessor George Osborne's economic policies. Hammond abandoned Osborne's plan to eliminate the deficit by 2020, announcing a tranche of spending policies that included borrowing £5 billion to build new houses. 'Make no mistake, fiscal consolidation must continue,' Hammond said, but he admitted it would proceed at a slower pace than previously planned.

4 October 2016
Steve Bell
Guardian

CREDIBILITY HITS NEW LOW...

An altercation between two UKIP MEPs resulted in one of them collapsing and being rushed to hospital. An image circulated online showing Steven Woolfe, the front-runner in the party's leadership contest, sprawled on a walkway in the European Parliament; there was speculation that he had been punched by a fellow MEP, Mike Hookem. The former UKIP leader Nigel Farage described the incident as 'one of those things that happens between men'.

7 October 2016
Peter Brookes
The Times

According to the cartoonist, 'The announcement of Diane Abbott as shadow home secretary caused some controversy and amusement. Many felt she was not well qualified for the post. However, the prospect of Donald Trump becoming president was even more ludicrous and, at the time, unlikely. This is a cartoon that carries a different significance in light of what's happened since. The glass of champagne was a mistake – I didn't know he was teetotal when I drew this.'

8 October 2016
Bob Moran
Daily Telegraph

10 October 2016
Morten Morland
The Times

Donald Trump was forced to apologise after a video emerged in which he bragged about sexually assaulting women. The 2005 video showed Trump saying he could approach beautiful women and 'grab them by the pussy' because he was famous: 'When you're a star they let you do it.' After a backlash, Trump retracted the comments, saying, 'Anyone who knows me knows these words don't reflect who I am.'

In her speech to the Conservative Party conference, Home Secretary Amber Rudd outlined new plans to limit immigration, including by forcing companies to reveal how many foreign staff they employed. After criticism of the so-called 'Rivers of Rudd' speech, Education Secretary Justine Greening appeared on television to announce an apparent government U-turn: 'This is not data that will be published. There will be absolutely no naming and shaming,' she said.

10 October 2016
Martin Rowson
Guardian

SICK PRANK

HM TREASURY

£66bn BREXIT

12 October 2016
Christian Adams
Daily Telegraph

A leaked Treasury report said that a 'hard Brexit' could cost £66 billion a year, with GDP falling by up to 10 per cent. The news caused former chancellor George Osborne to warn that the public had not voted to be 'poorer' when they chose to leave the EU, and that the government should aim to stay in the Single Market. Meanwhile, a craze spread across Britain involving people dressing as 'scary clowns' in an attempt to frighten unsuspecting members of the public.

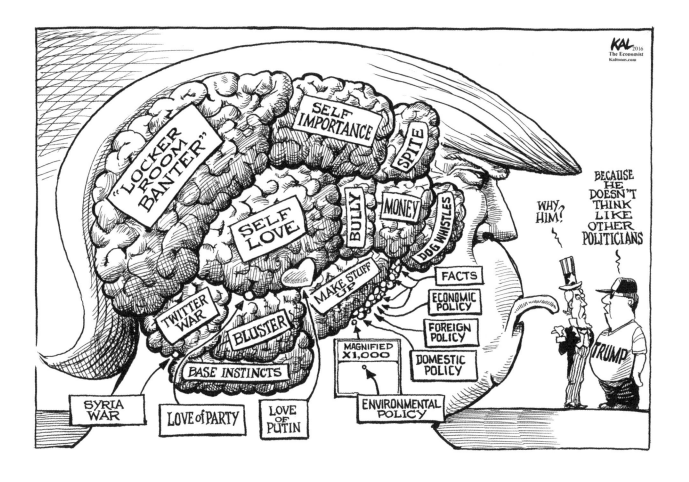

On 9 October 2016, Clinton and Trump went head to head at the second televised presidential debate. Trump had earlier endorsed claims that Hillary's husband Bill was a rapist, and that Clinton would be put 'in jail' if he became president. He also dismissed the sexually aggressive comments that had been revealed the previous week as normal 'locker room talk'.

13 October 2016
KAL
Economist

16 October 2016
Chris Riddell
Observer

Tesco temporarily stopped selling dozens of leading household brands due to a row with their manufacturer. The dispute developed when Unilever attempted to raise the prices of several products – including Marmite, Hellmann's mayonnaise and Pot Noodles – in response to the sharp drop in the value of the pound, following Britain's decision to leave the EU. Chris Riddell's cartoon plays on the 'love it or hate it' reputation of Marmite.

The *Sunday Times* printed a draft pro-EU article that the foreign secretary, Boris Johnson, had written before the Brexit referendum. The article caused speculation about whether Johnson had really supported leaving the EU, or had backed Brexit only for his own political gain. According to the cartoonist, 'Many believe his choice to take the Leave side was partially due to his own Machiavellian instincts that it could lead to him becoming PM; whether it was the best decision for the country was a separate, less important matter.'

17 October 2016
Ben Jennings
Guardian

According to the cartoonist, 'It was claimed that many adult refugees were gaining access to the UK by posing as children. Pictures surfaced of men who were clearly in their forties who had been admitted as minors. Controversially, the government suggested that all refugees be subjected to dental checks to determine their age. I was slightly nervous about covering such a sensitive story but I thought it would be fun to take the whole idea to extremes.'

23 October 2016
Bob Moran
Daily Telegraph

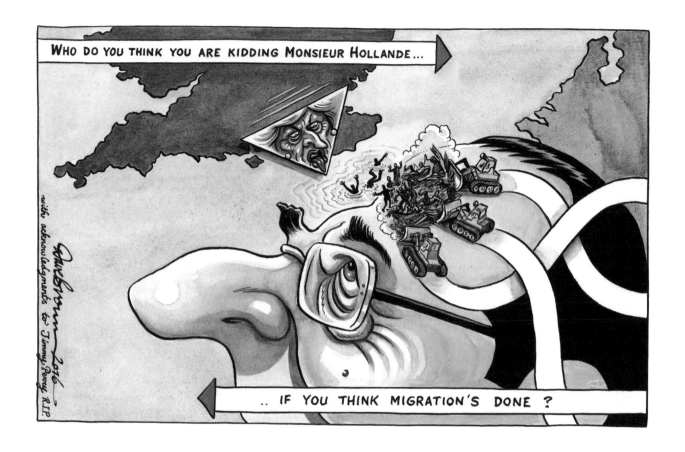

The French authorities bulldozed the 'Jungle' refugee camp in Calais and began relocating the migrants who lived there to other parts of the country. French President François Hollande called on the UK government to take in some of the 1,500 child migrants who had been living in the camp, but Theresa May refused – reminiscent, according to Dave Brown, of something from the classic Second World War sitcom *Dad's Army*.

25 October 2016
Dave Brown
Independent

26 October 2016
Christian Adams
Daily Telegraph

Theresa May had to face down dissent from within her own party after giving permission for a third runway to be built at Heathrow. The controversial move was described as 'catastrophic' by the high-profile Tory MP Zac Goldsmith, while cabinet ministers Boris Johnson and Justine Greening reiterated their opposition to the plans.

Jeremy Corbyn compared Theresa May to Baldrick, a character from the 1980s First World War comedy *Blackadder*. In the series, which famously ended with its characters going 'over the top', Baldrick was frequently mocked for his 'cunning plans' – similar, Corbyn said, to the government's 'cunning plan [of having] no plan' on Brexit.

27 October 2016
Steve Bell
Guardian

"Why, sometimes I've believed as many as six impossible things before Brexit..."

29 October 2016
Martin Rowson
Guardian

After Nissan announced extra investment in its Sunderland car factory, Theresa May came under fire for having made a 'secret deal' with the company. May was accused of having given 'assurances' that Brexit would have no effect on the trading conditions for the plant – a promise that critics said May could not possibly keep unless she had offered financial compensation to the company.

With only eleven days until the presidential election, Hillary Clinton's lead over Donald Trump collapsed after an intervention from the director of the FBI. James Comey announced that he was reopening the Bureau's investigation into Clinton's use of a private email server to send official correspondence. Donald Trump seized on the announcement as 'bigger than Watergate'.

31 October 2016
Christian Adams
Daily Telegraph

SOUTH YORKSHIRE CONSTABULARY OR DEATH

© Steve Bell 2016 · 4954 · 1 · 11 · 16 ~ Belltoons.co.uk ~

1 November 2016
Steve Bell
Guardian

Theresa May ruled out holding an inquiry into the Battle of Orgreave, the infamous clash between striking miners and the South Yorkshire Police during the 1984–5 Miners' Strike. The prime minister had previously hinted that she would consider investigating the incident, one of the most controversial moments of Margaret Thatcher's premiership. This cartoon mirrors the ending to the classic historical drama film *El Cid*, in which the dead body of the protagonist (played by Charlton Heston) is ridden on horseback into battle.

HEY! YOU!! GET ORFF MY CROWN!

AFTER TENNIEL

The High Court ruled that the government could not trigger Article 50, which formally began the Brexit process, without first consulting MPs. Downing Street criticised the verdict, arguing that the prime minister had the right to oversee the process. This cartoon references John Tenniel's illustration of the Queen of Hearts from *Alice in Wonderland*.

4 November 2016
Steve Bell
Guardian

5 November 2016
Bob Moran
Daily Telegraph

The press alleged that centrist parliamentarians and judges were trying to sabotage Britain's efforts to leave the EU. According to the cartoonist, 'With a team of politicians and judges conspiring to "thwart" Brexit, on the eve of Guy Fawkes night, I had no choice but to draw them as the gunpowder plotters. The image is based on the famous engraving by Crispijn van de Passe and it took a long time to draw!'

'I'm sorry to take so long. I can't make up my mind which one I loathe the least.'

Americans went to the polls on 8 November. The election was dubbed an 'unpopularity contest' after polls showed that Donald Trump and Hillary Clinton were the most unpopular pair of candidates in modern US history. On election day, Trump's ratings were thought slightly worse than Clinton's, with 61 per cent viewing him negatively compared with 52 per cent for her.

8 November 2016
Mac
Daily Mail

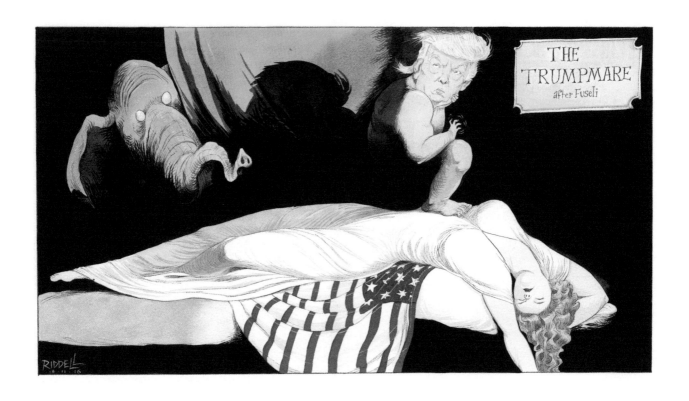

13 November 2016
Chris Riddell
Observer

In one of the biggest shocks in US political history, Donald Trump narrowly beat Hillary Clinton to be elected as the 45th president of the United States, following unexpected swings to the Republican nominee in Ohio, Pennsylvania and Florida. The president-elect told his supporters that he would 'bind the wounds of division' across America – a view not shared by this cartoon, which riffs on Henry Fuseli's 1781 painting *The Nightmare*.

According to the cartoonist, 'The first British politician to get a meeting with the newly elected American president and leader of the free world was Nigel Farage. Yes, UKIP's very own swivel-eyed bat-shit-crazy bigot. Not content with breaking the UK with Brexit, Farage now wanted to go and help destroy America.' The president-elect also took phone calls from Vladimir Putin and Theresa May.

14 November 2016
Brian Adcock
Independent

16 November 2016
KAL
Economist

The Obama administration reiterated its commitment to helping stop global warming, even as Donald Trump pledged to pull out of several major environmental agreements. Vice-President John Kerry said that the US government still supported the Paris Agreement, the 2015 treaty that pledged to curb emissions of greenhouse gases; but sources close to the president-elect said that he was trying to find ways to leave the agreement as quickly as possible.

In advance of Philip Hammond's Autumn Statement on the economy, Theresa May said that Britain's preparations to leave the EU were 'on track'. Meanwhile, Amazon Video broadcast the first episode of *The Grand Tour*, a new motoring show presented by the former faces of *Top Gear*: Jeremy Clarkson, Richard Hammond and James May.

19 November 2016
Martin Rowson
Guardian

WINDS OF CHANGE

20 November 2016
Bob Moran
Daily Telegraph

Philip Hammond said that he feared Donald Trump's protectionist policies could damage the global economy, but that he was sure Britain would have a 'very constructive dialogue with the new American administration'. According to the cartoonist, 'The UK was battered by storms as the world struggled to come to terms with the election of Donald Trump as president of the United States. This cartoon addresses the idea that Britain should view Trump as an exciting opportunity. Tell that to the poor cat.'

THE DASTARDLY ASSASSINATION IN THE THEATRE!!

151 years after Abraham Lincoln was assassinated during a play in Washington, D.C., controversy rocked the world of theatre again: Vice-President-elect Mike Pence was booed at a Broadway performance of hit musical *Hamilton*. At the end of the show, a cast member came on stage to read Pence a letter. 'We, sir, we are the diverse America who are alarmed and anxious that your new administration will not protect us,' he said. The incident angered Donald Trump, who tweeted, 'The cast of *Hamilton* was very rude last night to a very good man, Mike Pence. Apologize!'

21 November 2016
Martin Rowson
Guardian

21 November 2016
Steve Bright
Sun

Tony Blair announced his return to front-line politics, saying that he intended to be the figurehead of a new anti-Brexit group. Blair had previously described Brexit as a 'catastrophe' and called for a second referendum. The former prime minister's return to campaigning was welcomed by pro-Brexit MPs, who said he was still so hated that he would only increase public enthusiasm for leaving the EU – according to Steve Bright, a little like the deranged protagonist in the classic 1980 horror film *The Shining*.

Donald Trump continued to heap praise on former UKIP leader Nigel Farage, tweeting that 'Many people would like to see [Farage] represent Great Britain as their Ambassador to the United States. He would do a great job!' Farage said he was flattered by the tweet, calling it 'a bolt from the blue'. But Downing Street brushed off the suggestion: 'There is no vacancy as we already have an excellent ambassador to the United States,' said a spokesperson.

23 November 2016
Steve Bell
Guardian

43

Nicolas Sarkozy was knocked out of the race to be the right-wing Republican Party's candidate for the French presidency. The former president had run a pro-free-market, socially conservative campaign, but lost out in the first round of voting to both François Fillon and Alain Juppé. Sarkozy, who is 5'5", is well-known for wearing high heels that are designed to make him look taller.

HOMEMADE JAMS

with apologies to Lewis Carroll

In the Chancellor's Autumn Statement, the government outlined plans to help people who were 'just about managing' ('JAMs'). The proposals included increasing the minimum wage and constructing 40,000 new affordable homes. But some critics said that the policies were unaffordable and unachievable: this cartoon references Lewis Carroll's White Queen from *Through the Looking Glass*, who promises Alice 'jam tomorrow and jam yesterday – but never jam today'.

26 November 2016
Ingram Pinn
Financial Times

27 November 2016
Scott Clissold
Sunday Express

Dozens of retired professional footballers came forward to say they had been sexually abused by coaches when they were children. The first allegations were made in mid-November by Andy Woodward, a former defender for Sheffield United, who waived his right to anonymity to allege that he had been abused when he was a child footballer with Crewe Alexandra F.C. The Football Association announced an internal review on 27 November.

INTO THE ASHTRAY OF HISTORY...

Jeremy Corbyn hailed Fidel Castro as a 'champion of social justice' after the Cuban leader died at the age of 90. Although he admitted that Castro had 'flaws', Corbyn described him as 'a huge figure of modern history, national independence and 20th-century socialism'. Castro, who served as Cuba's leader from 1959 until his death, was known for his distinctive 'Cohiba' cigars.

28 November 2016
Morten Morland
The Times

3 December 2016
Martin Rowson
Guardian

The Liberal Democrats unexpectedly won in the Richmond Park by-election, overturning incumbent MP Zac Goldsmith's majority of 23,015. Goldsmith had stood as an independent candidate to protest against the government's backing of a third runway at the nearby Heathrow Airport. But Liberal Democrat Sarah Olney was able to capitalise on the constituency's strong anti-Brexit sentiment in order to defeat Goldsmith, who had supported the Leave campaign.

According to the cartoonist, 'Trump sparked a potentially damaging diplomatic row with China after speaking to Taiwanese president Tsai Ing-wen on the telephone, in a move experts said would anger Beijing. The call is thought to be the first between the leader of the island and a US president since ties between America and Taiwan were severed in 1979. Since then the US has adhered to the "one China" policy, which officially considers the independently governed island part of the same single Chinese nation as the mainland. Did Trump not give a damn for the way things are normally done, or was he being diplomatically naive? I think the former, and that is something I grudgingly like about him.'

4 December 2016
Brian Adcock
Independent

8 December 2016
Steve Bell
Guardian

Donald Trump was named by *Time* magazine as 'Person of the Year'. The magazine described Trump as 'President of the Divided States of America', concluding that 'because of Donald John Trump, whatever happens next, [America] will never be like it was before'. Trump was chosen from a shortlist that included Hillary Clinton, Vladimir Putin and Nigel Farage, who was credited with a crucial role in convincing Britain to leave the EU.

Footage emerged showing Boris Johnson, the foreign secretary, saying that Saudi Arabia was engaging in 'proxy wars' in the Middle East. The comments were particularly controversial because the prime minister had been trying to strengthen the relationship between the Saudi and British governments. A Downing Street spokesperson said the foreign secretary's comments were his personal views and did not reflect the position of the government.

11 December 2016
Chris Riddell
Observer

CHARM OFFENSIVE

17 December 2016
Ingram Pinn
Financial Times

A video emerged that seemed to show Theresa May looking isolated at a meeting of EU leaders. In the video, the prime minister stands alone and fidgets while other members of the summit chat. The incident was seized upon as evidence that Britain was being marginalised by European leaders as a result of Brexit.

Sajid Javid, the communities secretary, suggested that every public office holder should swear an oath of allegiance to 'British values'. Writing in the *Sunday Times*, Javid said that the pledge – which would apply to politicians, civil servants and council employees – would help build social cohesion. In the version of this cartoon printed in *The Times*, the title was changed from 'Oaf' to 'Oath' at the last minute because editors thought the former was too harsh.

19 December 2016
Morten Morland
The Times

THE BRIDGE ...

WELL ... MAYBE JUST THE FOUNDATIONS !

19 December 2016
Dave Brown
Independent

Nigel Farage said he wanted to be a 'bridge' between the UK government and Donald Trump's new administration. The former UKIP leader said he was well placed to help because of his good relationship with the president-elect and his connections with the Republican Party. Farage also alleged that Theresa May had banned the cabinet from working with him, and that this demonstrated how 'petty' British politics was.

Workers at Britain's railways, airlines and Post Offices all threatened to go on strike in the run-up to Christmas. Conductors at Southern Rail walked out for 48 hours to protest the introduction of automatic doors on trains, while Post Office employees downed tools for five days in response to branch closures. A strike by British Airways staff, meanwhile, was called off at the last minute when cabin crew came to an agreement with the management.

20 December 2016
Morten Morland
The Times

21 December 2016
Dave Brown
Independent

Nigel Farage caused controversy after seeming to blame German Chancellor Angela Merkel for a terror attack in Berlin. When a lorry killed 12 people by driving into a Christmas market, Farage tweeted, 'Terrible news from Berlin but no surprise. Events like these will be the Merkel legacy.'

Jamie Reed, one of Jeremy Corbyn's most prominent critics, resigned as an MP to take a job with the nuclear processing site in his constituency. Reed said that his goal was to serve his constituents, and that 'there's a better way of doing that in this community than to remain as a Member of Parliament'.

22 December 2016
Christian Adams
Daily Telegraph

Peace & Goodwill

BOB
24·12·16

24 December 2016
Bob Moran
Daily Telegraph

According to the cartoonist, 'In a concerning and unseasonal development in the close relationship between Vladimir Putin and President-elect Donald Trump, the two leaders called for their respective nations to boost their nuclear arsenals. I felt sad that the two men were making us all think about nuclear Armageddon so close to Christmas. Then I drew a cartoon that did exactly the same thing.'

PRESIDENTIAL GIFTS

According to the cartoonist, 'In a last-ditch attempt to protect environmental policies from Donald Trump, outgoing President Barack Obama issued an executive order permanently banning offshore oil and gas drilling in large areas of US Arctic waters. President Donald Trump, who appointed Rex Tillerson, ExxonMobil's chief executive, for his secretary of state, has since rescinded (possibly illegally) the ban. The issue has been taken up by environmental groups who have vowed to defend Obama's order in court.'

24 December 2016
Ingram Pinn
Financial Times

'I'm sorry you were upset, Ma'am. But there were parts of your Christmas speech we felt it prudent to edit out.'

28 December 2016
Mac
Daily Mail

The BBC's political editor, Laura Kuenssberg, said that a source had told her the Queen supported Brexit. Kuenssberg said that she had been informed in early 2016 that the Queen had 'told people at a private lunch that she thinks we should leave the EU'. Kuenssberg said her 'jaw hit the floor' when she was told the story.

Vladimir Putin denied that the Kremlin had used cyber attacks to interfere in the US presidential election. The CIA and the White House had alleged that Russian hackers had tried to sway American public opinion to secure a victory for Donald Trump; but a spokesman for the Russian government described the story as 'amusing rubbish that has no basis in fact'.

28 December 2016
KAL
Economist

Donald Trump tweeted his support for Israel, saying that the Obama administration had treated the nation with 'total disdain and disrespect'. Critics said that Trump's uncritical support for Israeli policy could undermine the two-state solution. According to the cartoonist, 'This cartoon was done during the post-Christmas doldrums, when it was difficult to avoid some kind of a seasonal link. I've always enjoyed drawing the three wise men. The religious connection is not too overt and there is a lot of comic potential in three pretentiously dressed chaps bouncing through the desert on the backs of camels, who, with their resentful and haughty faces are themselves a delight to draw.'

29 December 2016
Peter Schrank
Sunday Business Post

According to the cartoonist, 'Jeremy Corbyn accused Theresa May of behaving like Henry VIII or a similar autocratic monarch because of her refusal to put a final Brexit deal to a vote in Parliament. The Labour leader insisted that the prime minister could not be allowed to use the royal prerogative to bypass the Commons over the UK's future relationship with continental Europe. With May feeling confident due to her polling very high it was not hard to imagine her as the bombastic king.'

30 December 2016
Brian Adcock
Independent

An increase in rail fares led to accusations that private rail companies were exploiting Britain's commuters. Following criticism from the Labour Party, Transport Secretary Chris Grayling pointed to the government's rail modernisation programme, saying it had 'always fairly balanced' the cost of Britain's railways between taxpayers and passengers. According to the cartoonist, 'Despite experiencing a less frequent and more overcrowded service, rail commuters were once again squeezed and required to pay more for the privilege of travelling on our sub-standard rail network. Fares went up by an average of 2.3 per cent and as usual it's the fat cats who get the cream.'

3 January 2017
Brian Adcock
Independent

'Yes. A lot better, thank you. Luckily Philip has managed to avoid it.'

Princess Anne reassured the public that the Queen was 'feeling better' after a 'heavy cold' meant she missed the New Year's Day church service at Sandringham. Rumours circulated that the Queen had died following a spoof by a fake BBC news account, which tweeted, 'BREAKING: Buckingham Palace announces the death of Queen Elizabeth II at the age of 90.' The account was later suspended, but not before social media users began speculating that a 'media blackout' was trying to cover up the news.

3 January 2017
Mac
Daily Mail

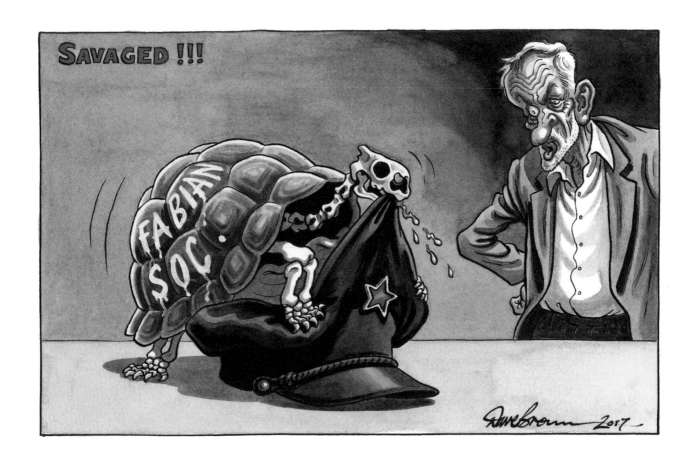

SAVAGED !!!

4 January 2017
Dave Brown
Independent

The left-wing think tank the Fabian Society said the Labour Party was 'too weak' to win a general election by itself. The society, which is affiliated with Labour, warned that Jeremy Corbyn was on track to return fewer than 200 MPs in a general election. The tortoise in this cartoon refers to the Fabians' logo, which represents the society's commitment to a slow, steady transition to socialism.

According to the cartoonist, this drawing refers to 'the UK's ridiculous stance on the Brexit negotiations, with no clear plan or preparations for what Brexit will be'. He says, 'I imagined this as a hostage situation, where the perpetrator has already entered the building and been surrounded but has no idea what their demands are. The guy I depicted in the building is Sir Tim Barrow, the British diplomat who will have a key role in the negotiations. This was a popular cartoon with Remainers and an unpopular one with Brexiteers, naturally.'

6 January 2017
Ben Jennings
Guardian

INTELLIGENCE

7 January 2017
Ingram Pinn
Financial Times

In advance of a meeting with US intelligence officials, Donald Trump implied that the CIA and the FBI were struggling to find evidence of Russian interference in the presidential election. He wrote on Twitter, 'The "Intelligence" briefing on so-called "Russian hacking" was delayed until Friday, perhaps more time needed to build a case. Very strange!' Senior intelligence officials denied his suggestion, saying the day of the meeting had not changed.

Theresa May wrote an article for the *Sunday Telegraph* outlining her vision for a 'shared society', reminiscent of David Cameron's earlier promise of a 'big society'. The Labour Party said that May's comments rang hollow, with Jeremy Corbyn joking that the phrase meant 'more people sharing hospital corridors on trolleys'. The cartoonist says, 'A shared society, from a Tory! For a split second I almost believed her and fantasised that these Conservatives were somehow different, and that perhaps the fundamental soulless values of "I'm alright Jack", "worship wealth before all else" and unenlightened greedy individualism were changing in the very core of the Conservative Party! I am a gullible pillock sometimes.'

9 January 2017
Brian Adcock
Independent

RELAUNCH ... IN A WAGE CAP

11 January 2017
Dave Brown
Independent

Jeremy Corbyn 'relaunched' his leadership of the Labour Party, using a series of speeches to outline several new policies. The Tories dubbed the event a 'day of chaos' after Corbyn was forced into a series of U-turns. Most controversially, he floated the idea that there should be a cap on the wages of high earners during a speech in the morning, but then made no mention of the policy in a speech that afternoon.

A leaked US intelligence dossier alleged that the Kremlin had evidence of lurid details about Donald Trump's sex life. According to the cartoonist, rumours that Vladimir Putin had videos of Trump participating in a 'urinating sex orgy' were good news for satirists: 'It seemed like where 2016 was the year of outsider victories and celebrity deaths, 2017 might be the year of hyper-surrealism. Whether the story had any truth in it, who knows! We're awash with fake news these days, along with people claiming real news is fake news, so it's hard to know what's real anymore. However, the fact that Trump appeared to idolise Putin was certainly true, so the urination metaphor was a *golden* opportunity . . .'

14 January 2017
Ben Jennings
i

14 January 2017
Peter Brookes
The Times

Labour MP Tristram Hunt resigned from Parliament to take up the position of director at the Victoria & Albert Museum in London. Hunt had been one of the Labour leader's most outspoken critics, but said that his disagreement with Jeremy Corbyn and his allies 'wasn't the spur for stepping down'. Here, Corbyn and his allies Seumas Milne and Diane Abbott replace the three graces of Antonio Canova's famous sculpture – one of the star exhibits in the V&A.

Donald Trump told Theresa May that 'Brexit is going to be a wonderful thing for your country,' and said that he supported the break-up of the EU. The news came just after May announced that Britain was heading for a 'hard Brexit', and that it would be leaving the Single Market in order to regain control of immigration.

17 January 2017
Christian Adams
Daily Telegraph

22 January 2017
Bob Moran
Daily Telegraph

Donald Trump was sworn in as the 45th president of the United States. Within hours of entering the Oval Office, Trump issued a series of executive orders that denounced several of Barack Obama's key policies. According to the cartoonist, 'Donald Trump's first 24 hours in office seemed to focus on his intention to destroy the legacy of Barack Obama. Trump was behaving as though he had just toppled some evil dictator. Hence the cartoon.'

'No, M'lud. The first round was from the Lib Dems, then Nicola Sturgeon – this one's from Jeremy Corbyn.'

The Supreme Court ruled that Theresa May had to consult Parliament before starting the process of leaving the EU. The judges' verdict concluded that the government 'cannot trigger Article 50 without an Act of Parliament'. The news was welcomed by opposition parties, with a Labour spokesperson saying it would help ensure that the government was 'accountable to Parliament' during Brexit negotiations.

25 January 2017
Mac
Daily Mail

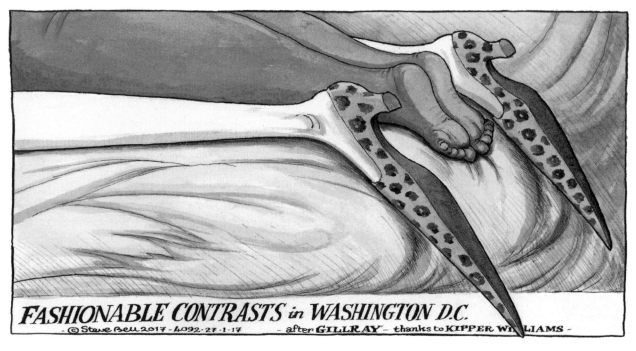

FASHIONABLE CONTRASTS in WASHINGTON D.C.
- © Steve Bell 2017 - 4092. 27.1.17   - after GILLRAY - thanks to KIPPER WILLIAMS -

Theresa May visited Washington for her first meeting with Donald Trump at the White House. The prime minister said she looked forward to building a strong personal relationship with the new president. The cartoon is a pastiche of James Gillray's *Fashionable Contrasts; – or – the Duchess's Little Shoe Yielding to the Magnitude of the Duke's Foot*, (right) published in 1792. The original print depicted the Duke and Duchess of York's legs in a sexually suggestive position, with the Duchess's feet drawn comically small – a poke at the press's obsequiousness about her 'elegant' footwear.

27 January 2017
Steve Bell
Guardian

Theresa May attended a formal lunch with Donald Trump in the White House's banqueting room. She reiterated the British government's opposition to torture after Donald Trump said that he supported waterboarding terror suspects. 'When ISIS is doing things that nobody has ever heard of since medieval times . . . we have to fight fire with fire,' the president had said in a TV interview.

28 January 2017
Peter Brookes
The Times

31 January 2017
Steve Bell
Guardian

A former head of the Foreign Office said that Theresa May's decision to invite Donald Trump for an official visit had put the Queen in a 'very difficult position'. The formal state visit would involve the Queen acting as Trump's host. In a letter to *The Times*, Lord Ricketts said, 'It would have been far wiser to wait to see what sort of president he would turn out to be before advising the Queen to invite him.'

The Labour Party's policy on Brexit descended into confusion when Jeremy Corbyn made statements that suggested he was unsure of the party's stance on Article 50. Corbyn had previously said that all Labour MPs would be obliged to vote in favour of triggering the clause, which would formally begin the process of leaving the EU. But after a major revolt by MPs and shadow ministers, Corbyn's aides said that he was still making up his mind. One MP said that the party was in 'utter chaos', commenting, 'Even Labour MPs don't understand what our position is.'

1 February 2017
Dave Brown
Independent

FAMILY BUSINESS

4 February 2017
Ingram Pinn
Financial Times

Donald Trump gave control of his business empire over to his two sons for the duration of his presidency. The president had faced allegations that there was a conflict of interest between being head of state and running private businesses. His critics said that the decision to hand management of the businesses to Donald Trump Jr. and Eric Trump was insufficient, and that the president should have placed his assets in a blind trust.

According to the cartoonist, 'Donald Trump signed an executive order on 27 January banning citizens of seven majority-Muslim countries – Iran, Iraq, Libya, Somalia, Sudan, Syria and Yemen – from the US, temporarily suspending America's refugee programme and barring Syrian refugees from the country indefinitely. President Trump experienced an early embarrassing knockback when a federal judge in Seattle, James Robart, ruled that the order be suspended temporarily "on a nationwide basis" – meaning government officials had to stop enforcing it, and once-banned travellers could enter the country – on the grounds that the order was causing "immediate and irreparable injury" and therefore may be ruled unconstitutional. When the Donald is upset, normally his first response is to vent his spleen on Twitter. The orange man-baby didn't disappoint.'

5 February 2017
Brian Adcock
Independent

NUMBER ONE...

7 February 2017
Morten Morland
The Times

Fighting intensified in Syria throughout February, with rebel forces increasingly put on a back foot by Bashar Al-Assad's troops' offensive. Amnesty International estimated that the Syrian regime had authorised the execution of 13,000 prisoners in a single military jail between 2011 and 2015.

House of Commons Speaker John Bercow said he would oppose Donald Trump giving a speech to Parliament on a state visit to the UK. 'An address by a foreign leader to both houses of Parliament is not an automatic right, it is an earned honour,' Bercow said, pointing to Trump's migrant ban as evidence that he should not be invited. Backbench Tory MPs criticised Bercow for the intervention, with one branding his comments 'unwise'.

8 February 2017
Christian Adams
Daily Telegraph

According to the cartoonist, 'I think these were some of the darkest days for the Jeremy Corbyn-led Labour Party. Droves of top MPs had resigned and it seemed increasingly difficult for JC to put together a credible shadow cabinet. At this point I thought Corbyn's days were numbered and the chances of seeing a Labour government any time soon were slim. You don't always know exactly how cartoons are going to turn out and this one seemed to capture the mood around the state of the Labour Party at the time, at least from my point of view, and it made me quite sad.'

12 February 2017
Brian Adcock
Independent

Newly released figures showed a spike in waiting times at A&E in NHS hospitals. According to the cartoonist, 'I drew this cartoon in response to Theresa May and the government saying they were spending more on the NHS yet being contradicted by pictures on TV of groaning, overloaded hospital A&E departments.'

12 February 2017
David Simonds
Observer

Dropping the pilot

Michael Flynn resigned as Donald Trump's national security adviser after the president told him that an 'eroding level of trust' made his position untenable. He was forced to quit after it emerged that he had had discussed sanctions with the Russian ambassador before Trump took office, and had then misled Vice-President Mike Pence on the issue. The cartoon is a pastiche of Sir John Tenniel's *Dropping the Pilot* (right), published in 1890, which commented on the forced resignation of Otto von Bismarck from the government of Kaiser Wilhelm II.

15 February 2017
Martin Rowson
Guardian

UKIP leader Paul Nuttall was forced to apologise after his website falsely claimed that he had lost friends in the Hillsborough disaster. He said that although he had known people who died, he was 'very sorry' that he had led people to think he was close to any of the 96 victims. Relatives of those killed reacted angrily to the apology, with Margaret Aspinall of the Hillsborough Family Support Group describing Nuttall's claims as 'an insult'.

16 February 2017
Dave Brown
Independent

'He insists they all have a compartment. The last one had
two aunts, three cousins and the window cleaner in it.'

16 February 2017
Mac
Daily Mail

North Korea tested a ballistic missile for the first time since Donald Trump had become president. The previous month the North Korean premier, Kim Jong-un, had warned that his army was nearly capable of launching long-range missiles that could reach North America. The missile, which landed in the sea between Korea and Japan, was fired just a day after Trump had met Japanese Prime Minister Shinzō Abe, and pledged to work with Japan to tackle the threat from North Korea.

Tony Blair said he wanted the British people to 'rise up' and change their minds on Brexit. He warned that the UK was on a 'rush over the cliff's edge', but that he was on a 'mission' to change the public's mind. Blair's supporters praised his 'heroic' intervention – here he is depicted as Liberty in Eugène Delacroix's painting *Liberty Leading the People* – but Boris Johnson criticised the former prime minister. 'I urge the British people to rise up and turn off the TV next time Blair comes on with his condescending campaign,' the foreign secretary said.

18 February 2017
Martin Rowson
Guardian

21 February 2017
Morten Morland
The Times

In a break with parliamentary convention, Theresa May sat in the House of Lords to watch peers discuss the Brexit bill. According to a spokesperson, the prime minister decided to sit on the steps of the royal throne during the debate 'in recognition of the importance of this bill'. Although prime ministers are entitled to enter the Lords, the move is unprecedented in recent history – leading to accusations that May had adopted a Clint Eastwood-style swagger in her dealings with peers.

Boris Johnson was accused of insensitivity after telling a summit of European politicians that Brexit would mean 'liberation' from the EU. A Swedish MEP told the foreign secretary that 'the word "liberation" in the history of Europe has a very strong meaning', and that his comments were in 'bad taste'. Meanwhile, Sutton United FC's reserve goalkeeper, Wayne Shaw, resigned after the Gambling Commission and the Football Association confirmed they were investigating him. He had come under fire for eating a pie on the bench while knowing that a gambling company was offering odds on him doing so during a match with Arsenal.

23 February 2017
Peter Brookes
The Times

ELECTORAL STORMS

25 February 2017
Ingram Pinn
Financial Times

The Conservatives won a historic victory in the Copeland by-election, gaining a seat that Labour had held since the 1930s. In the Stoke by-election, however, Labour's Gareth Snell held the seat easily, seeing off a bid by UKIP leader Paul Nuttall to become MP. Meanwhile, Storm Doris brought snow, rain and winds as high as 90 miles per hour to the UK.

The Conservative peer Michael Heseltine announced he would rebel against Theresa May's Brexit bill. He said he was backing an opposition amendment calling for MPs to be given a vote on the deal reached at the end of Brexit negotiations. On the same day, Jeremy Corbyn vowed to 'turn back the Tory tide' in the wake of Labour's disastrous result in the Copeland by-election.

27 February 2017
Martin Rowson
Guardian

THE KIPPER SLAPPING DANCE...

with acknowledgments to Monty Python

1 March 2017
Dave Brown
Independent

Nigel Farage publicly denounced UKIP's sole MP, Douglas Carswell, as a 'Tory party posh boy' who was 'consumed with jealousy and a desire to hurt me'. The former party leader accused Carswell of deliberately undermining his chances of being awarded a knighthood. Commentators said the Kippers' infighting was turning UKIP into a farce; this cartoon refers to the surreal *Monty Python* sketch 'The Fish-Slapping Dance'.

SNP leader Nicola Sturgeon called for a second referendum on Scottish independence. According to the cartoonist, 'The cartoon is about the irony of Theresa May's speech at the Scottish Tory Party conference, where she told the Scottish government to stop "obsessing" about independence and get on with the day job.'

3 March 2017
Steven Camley
Scottish Herald

6 March 2017
KAL
Economist

American newspapers alleged that several of President Trump's allies – including his son-in-law Jared Kushner and Attorney General Jeff Sessions – had met with senior Russian diplomats during the election campaign. Trump said that the allegations of Russian involvement in his campaign were a 'total witch-hunt', adding that Democrats had 'lost their grip on reality'.

SELECTIVE EDUCATION

Theresa May outlined plans to spend a further £320 million on the government's free school programme, paving the way for the foundation of several new grammar schools. In the budget, Chancellor Philip Hammond said that the investment was part of the government's plan to open 500 new free schools by 2020, many of which would use such selection methods as the 11 plus.

7 March 2017
Nicola Jennings
Guardian

THE UNVEILING ...

The Queen unveiled a memorial to British forces who served during the wars in Iraq and Afghanistan. The centrepiece of the statue, designed by Paul Day, is a bronze casting of a group of soldiers in combat gear. The opening ceremony's organisers were condemned for inviting former prime minister Tony Blair to attend, just months after the Iraq Inquiry criticised his use of a dubious intelligence document (the so-called 'dodgy dossier') to make the case for war.

10 March 2017
Dave Brown
Independent

According to the cartoonist, this cartoon references a widely published photo from Prime Minister's Questions: 'Theresa May chuckling like some demonic pelican swallowing a fish whole.' He adds, 'I decided to rework it so that she was devouring the 2015 Tory manifesto that the government (at that point) had been elected on, which Mrs May was dismissing many of the key pledges from.'

11 March 2017
Ben Jennings
i

STARTING PISTOLS AT DAWN...

14 March 2017
Morten Morland
The Times

Theresa May said that Nicola Sturgeon was 'playing politics' over Scottish independence, warning her that 'politics is not a game'. The prime minister made the comments after the SNP leader called for a second independence referendum, suggesting that it would give the Scottish public a choice between May's Brexit deal and remaining in the EU.

DUTCH DEFENCES

The anti-immigration Party for Freedom (PVV) was comprehensively defeated in the Dutch general election. The party's leader, Geert Wilders, accepted defeat after his party finished a distant second to Mark Rutte's People's Party for Freedom and Democracy (VVD). The re-election of the centre-right government was hailed as a victory against the rising tide of right-wing populism in Europe.

18 March 2017
Ingram Pinn
Financial Times

19 March 2017
Scott Clissold
Sunday Express

The former chancellor, George Osborne, was appointed editor of the *London Evening Standard*. Osborne, who had been sacked by Theresa May when she became prime minister, said that under his editorship the newspaper would be 'fearless' in scrutinising the government. But critics said that Osborne was hoping to undermine May's Brexit plan by creating a 'new power base' in journalism.

According to the cartoonist, 'As sports fans were enjoying the Six Nations rugby tournament, former prime minister Gordon Brown called for Scotland to be granted more political independence post-Brexit. With Nicola Sturgeon continuing to press for a second independence referendum, it seemed that Theresa May was having to defend the Union on two fronts.'

19 March 2017
Bob Moran
Sunday Telegraph

PEACEMAKER...

22 March 2017
Peter Brookes
The Times

Martin McGuinness, the former IRA leader and deputy first minister of Northern Ireland, died aged 66. The Sinn Féin politician was hailed for his role in bringing peace to Ireland, having played a central role in the power-sharing government that brought an end to the Troubles. But critics said that McGuiness's involvement in the paramilitary group the Provisional IRA during the 1970s and 1980s made him a terrorist.

A viral social media image that mocks Britain's Brexit strategy by comparing it to *The Adventures of Tintin* was spotted in a European Council meeting room. In the image, Tintin panics as Captain Haddock burns their boat's oars, alongside the caption 'Tintin and the Brexit Plan'. A Brussels source noticed the satirical poster hanging in the EU Brexit task force's 'war room' – although in the original, Tintin is not escaping on a lifeboat.

23 March 2017
Christian Adams
Daily Telegraph

23 March 2017
Steve Bell
Guardian

Five people died and 50 were injured in a terrorist attack in Westminster. Khalid Masood drove a car into pedestrians on Westminster Bridge, then stabbed a police officer near the gates of the Houses of Parliament, before being shot dead by armed police. Masood had said in a final text message that the attack was an act of jihad in revenge for Western military action in the Middle East.

ARTICLE 50 HAND-DELIVERED BY BARROW...

Theresa May signed the letter that triggered Article 50, giving official notice to European Council President Donald Tusk that Britain would leave the EU. The letter was hand-delivered by Tim Barrow, Britain's ambassador to the EU. May later told Parliament that the delivery of the letter marked 'the moment for the country to come together'.

29 March 2017
Dave Brown
Independent

29 March 2017
Steve Bell
Guardian

A *Daily Mail* front page was branded sexist for running the headline 'Never mind Brexit, who won Legs-it!' next to a photo of Theresa May and Nicola Sturgeon. According to the accompanying article by Sarah Vine, the photo showed that Sturgeon's legs were 'tantalisingly crossed . . . a direct attempt at seduction'. In response, Steve Bell decided to remind the public of another infamous moment in the *Mail*'s history – when its proprietor, Lord Rothermere, was photographed with Adolf Hitler in 1934.

'Forget it. From now on my headache is permanent!'

The healthcare regulator outlined plans to make Viagra, the drug used to treat erectile dysfunction, available over the counter at chemists. Previously the pill had only been obtainable with a doctor's prescription. Meanwhile, the NHS announced cost-cutting plans that included making patients pay for basic items such as painkillers, hay fever drugs and indigestion tablets.

29 March 2017
Mac
Daily Mail

Boris Johnson said the UK would 'stand up for Gibraltar' in the face of 'unacceptable' Spanish lobbying for the small territory to become a part of Spain. According to the cartoonist, 'I remember finding it difficult to come up with an image that could combine Spain, the issue of Gibraltar and angry Boris Johnson. I went through several rejected roughs featuring monkeys and the Gibraltar rock before realising Boris would work well as a big shaggy bull.'

2 April 2017
Bob Moran
Daily Telegraph

GREAT BRITISH EASTER EGG HUNT...

Human rights campaigners criticised Theresa May's Easter trade visit to Riyadh in Saudi Arabia, saying she was helping fuel a humanitarian crisis. The UK frequently sells arms to the Saudi government, which is using its military to help quash a rebellion in neighbouring Yemen. May defended the trip, saying that the UK would be 'raising the humanitarian issue' during negotiations.

5 April 2017
Dave Brown
Independent

The Labour Party suspended former mayor of London Ken Livingstone from holding office for a year after he made controversial comments about Hitler and Zionism. Livingstone had said that Hitler had been 'supporting Zionism before he went mad and ended up killing 6 million Jews'. A Labour disciplinary panel ruled that his comments had been 'grossly detrimental to the party'. Jeremy Corbyn condemned Livingstone's comments, but several Labour MPs criticised the leadership for allowing Livingstone to remain a member of the party at all.

6 April 2017
Morten Morland
The Times

ORANGE LINE

The United States launched a missile attack on an airbase in Syria. The strike was in retaliation for Bashar Al-Assad's use of nerve gas on his own citizens a few days previously. Some commentators were surprised that President Trump had authorised the attack: it antagonised Syria's allies in the Kremlin, who allegedly hold compromising information on the president. But the orange-tanned president said the attack was necessary because the use of chemical weapons had 'crossed a lot of lines'.

9 April 2017
Chris Riddell
Observer

PASSENGER DRAGGED FROM G7 UNITED AIRLINES...

12 April 2017
Peter Brookes
The Times

Foreign Secretary Boris Johnson failed to persuade members of the G7 group of nations to impose sanctions on Russia, in response to its continued support for the Syrian regime, but the proposals were rejected by representatives of the other major powers. Meanwhile, a video of an injured passenger being dragged off an overbooked United Airlines plane by security guards went viral on social media.

The American military dropped the largest non-nuclear bomb in its arsenal on an Islamic State tunnel complex in Afghanistan, just days after a US air strike on a base in Syria. Donald Trump said he was 'very proud' of his forces' use of the so-called 'mother of all bombs'. According to the cartoonist, 'I don't think I was the only cartoonist to portray Trump in this way at Easter. First I tried to draw it without showing any of his hair, but as soon as you do that it isn't Donald Trump any more. I made his fringe stick out from under the hood and suddenly it was him again.'

15 April 2017
Bob Moran
Daily Telegraph

17 April 2017
Brian Adcock
Independent

A North Korean missile test failed seconds after it was fired, possibly as a result of US interference. According to the cartoonist, 'Not long after America – under the worrying leadership of Donald Trump – bombed a Syrian airfield, North Korea – under the bizarre leadership of Kim Jong-un – tested their first ballistic missile. Unfortunately for fruitcake Kim, it wasn't quite as successful as President Trump's first military outing.'

Turkish President Tayyip Erdoğan claimed victory in a referendum on whether to grant him sweeping new powers. Erdoğan said that replacing the parliamentary system with a president-led executive would allow the country to 'modernise'. But his critics said that the referendum would allow him to crush dissent and commit human rights abuses.

18 April 2017
Morten Morland
The Times

19 April 2017
Christian Adams
Daily Telegraph

Theresa May called a snap election for 8 June. In a statement delivered from Number 10, the prime minister said, 'I have concluded the only way to guarantee certainty and security for years ahead is to hold this election.' Even though Labour was trailing badly in the polls, Jeremy Corbyn welcomed the decision, saying that it provided an opportunity to elect a government that would 'put the interests of the majority first'.

Echoing Kaa, the snake in *The Jungle Book*, Theresa May called on voters to 'trust in me' to deal with Brexit. According to the cartoonist, 'This image, inspired by one of my favourite films, sums up for me the fundamental problem with the 2017 election: we, the voters, were encouraged to endorse the Conservatives to strengthen Theresa May's hand in negotiating the UK's exit from the EU. Yet we didn't know what sort of exit she had in mind. Considering the seriousness of the danger facing the country this was a frightening prospect.'

23 April 2017
Peter Schrank
Sunday Business Post

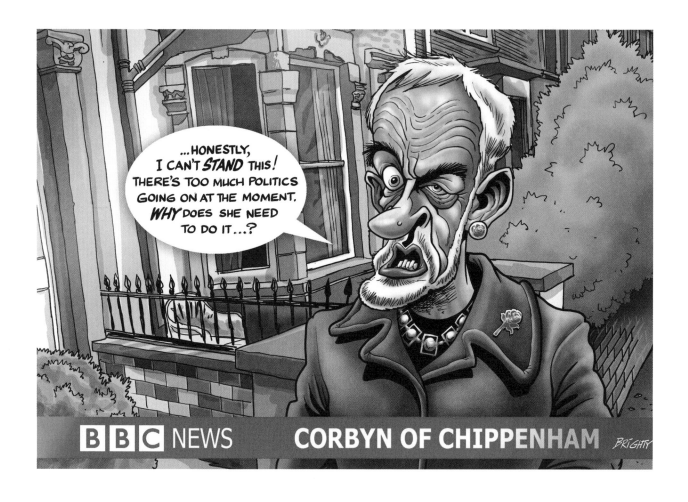

24 April 2017
Steve Bright
Sun

A 75-year-old woman, 'Brenda from Bristol', became an unlikely viral phenomenon when she expressed her exasperation at Theresa May's decision to call an election. 'You're joking, not another one?' she asked BBC News. 'I honestly can't stand this. There's too much politics going on at the moment – why does she need to do it?' Meanwhile, the turmoil in Jeremy Corbyn's Labour Party showed no sign of abating in the wake of the announcement.

Emmanuel Macron got through to the second round of the French presidential election. His victory meant he would face the far-right Front National candidate Marine Le Pen for the presidency. As a centrist candidate without the backing of a major party, Macron's victory marked the first time in 60 years that neither of France's main left- or right-wing parties made it through to the final stage of voting.

25 April 2017
Dave Brown
Independent

THE CREATION OF FARRON...

26 April 2017
Peter Brookes
The Times

Liberal Democrat leader Tim Farron said that he did not believe gay sex is a sin, after questions about his stance on homosexuality threatened to damage his party's election campaign. Farron, a committed Christian, had previously refused to discuss the matter, prompting allegations that he held homophobic views. He now said that he had evaded the question because he did not think politicians should comment on theological matters.

The plan to build a 'Garden Bridge' over the River Thames backed by the former mayor of London Boris Johnson was derailed by his successor, Sadiq Khan. Khan said that the project risked leaving taxpayers with higher bills, and that he would not offer financial guarantees for the structure. Theresa May, meanwhile, was ridiculed for repeating the phrase 'strong and stable government' dozens of times in a series of election campaign appearances.

29 April 2017
Martin Rowson
Guardian

29 April 2017
Ben Jennings
i

UKIP leader Paul Nuttall reiterated his support for a ban on the niqab and the burka in public spaces. In his party's election manifesto, Islamic facial coverings were described as 'barriers to integration' and 'dehumanising symbols of segregation'. But at a press conference, a UKIP spokesperson said that the ban would not apply to 'big hats' or nuns' veils.

Former prime minister David Cameron installed a £25,000 'luxury shed' in his garden, saying it would be a good place to write his memoirs. Theresa May, on the other hand, was having a less relaxing time: she came under fire for continuing to repeat the catchphrase 'strong and stable' while campaigning, and the Labour Party attacked her government for failing to keep houses' rental costs down while in power.

2 May 2017
Martin Rowson
Guardian

As the fourth series of the BBC's hit police drama *Line of Duty* came to an end, Labour frontbenchers including Jeremy Corbyn, John McDonnell and Diane Abbott came under fire for their policing policy. Abbott, the shadow home secretary, in particular was ridiculed after a 'car-crash interview' on LBC Radio: she pledged to employ an extra 10,000 police officers, but seemed unsure of how much the policy would cost, at first estimating a price tag of £300,000, before revising it upwards to £80 million while live on air.

3 May 2017
Peter Brookes
The Times

EU negotiators revised the so-called 'Brexit Bill' for the UK government up to €100 billion, even though European Commission President Jean-Claude Juncker had previously told Theresa May that the cost of leaving the EU would be around €60 billion. Back in Britain, the Tories launched a poster that included an image of a 'tax bombshell', alleging that a Labour government would bring 'more debt, higher taxes'. According to the cartoonist, 'This cartoon was unpublished as it was superseded by the news that Prince Philip had retired from public life. This is one of the perils of working for an evening newspaper where the deadline is 11am.'

4 May 2017
Christian Adams
London Evening Standard
(unpublished)

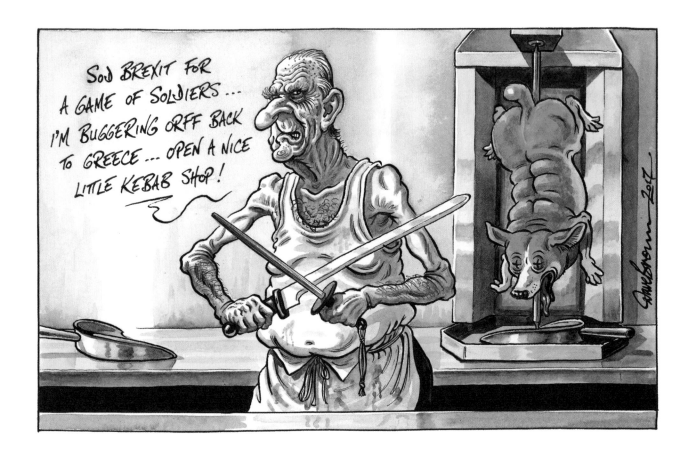

5 May 2017
Dave Brown
Independent

Prince Philip announced he was retiring at the age of 95. The Duke of Edinburgh had been a central figure in public life since he moved to the UK from Greece in 1947, endearing himself to the British public with his gaffe-prone sense of humour and frank opinions – which supposedly include a hatred of the Queen's corgis.

Emmanuel Macron, the pro-EU centrist candidate for president of France, defeated his far-right opponent Marine Le Pen in the final round of voting. Macron's victory, which ended decades of rule by two well-established parties, was seen as a blow to the far right across Europe. Le Pen thanked the 11 million people who had voted for her and the Front National, and said the election had revealed the depth of the division between 'patriots and globalists' in France.

8 May 2017
Christian Adams
London Evening Standard

ELECTION LAUNCH...

WE'RE GONNA NEED A BIGGER VOTE!

10 May 2017
Dave Brown
Independent

At the Labour Party's formal election campaign launch in Manchester, Jeremy Corbyn admitted that it would be a major challenge to overturn the Tories' poll lead before the general election. As this *Jaws*-themed cartoon suggests, Corbyn had come under sustained attacks from Rupert Murdoch's newspapers, Theresa May's Conservatives and 'fat cat' lobby groups: surveys of public opinion suggested Labour was on track for a historic defeat.

The *Daily Telegraph* obtained a leaked version of the Labour manifesto, which the newspaper said 'would take the UK back to the 1970s' if implemented. Jeremy Corbyn's policies included renationalising the railways, scrapping tuition fees and hiking up corporation tax. Meanwhile, Labour politicians attacked Theresa May for saying she had 'always been in favour' of legalising fox hunting, and for promising a parliamentary vote on the issue in the Conservative manifesto.

12 May 2017
Steve Bell
Guardian

14 May 2017
Chris Riddell
Observer

Commentators contrasted the Labour Party's populist left-wing manifesto with the Conservatives' hardline policies on immigration, fox hunting and Brexit. One article in the *Independent* described Theresa May as the 'Cruella de Vil of the Tories', after the fur-wearing villain from the Disney film *One Hundred and One Dalmations*.

Vladimir Putin appeared to mock Donald Trump for sharing classified information with the Russian ambassador to the US. Trump had reportedly let slip confidential US intelligence during a meeting between American and Russian diplomats in the Oval Office. Russian state media published a video of Putin and his foreign minister, Sergey Lavrov, sharing a joke about the alleged gaffe.

18 May 2017
KAL
Economist

19 May 2017
Patrick Blower
Daily Telegraph

Theresa May launched the Conservative Party's manifesto. Its proposals included increasing NHS funding, amending the funding model of social care, and committing the Tories to 'strong and stable government'. In the Q&A following her speech, May compared herself to Margaret Thatcher: 'Thatcher was a Conservative, I'm a Conservative, [and] this is a Conservative manifesto,' she said.

The Tories' plan to reform social care funding was condemned as a 'dementia tax' that would punish the elderly. According to the cartoonist, 'This was the first sign that the election campaign was not going as Theresa May had hoped, and it was going to get a lot worse. May and her fellow Tory cohorts' repetition of the "strong and stable" mantra was hugely irritating and condescending and the satirists were not going to let them get away with it. The Tories were lampooned for it endlessly and had to eventually reduce the amount it was used or stop saying it altogether, which gave me great pleasure. "Wrong and painful" was my attempt at undermining "strong and stable", but it never caught on – unlike the better "weak and wobbly".'

22 May 2017
Brian Adcock
Independent

Blower
24·5·17
after
Lowry

24 May 2017
Patrick Blower
Daily Telegraph

A terrorist attack in Manchester left 23 people dead. Salman Ramadan Abedi detonated a homemade bomb as families were leaving a concert by the singer Ariana Grande at Manchester Arena. In the wake of the attack, messages of support poured in from around the world praising the city's resilience and culture – including this tribute to the great Mancunian painter L. S. Lowry.

AN AMERICAN IN BRUSSELS

A video from the NATO conference showed Donald Trump shoving the prime minister of Montenegro out of the way during a photocall. The moment came during a summit in which Donald Trump criticised his allies for paying too little towards NATO's budget, and which involved clashes over his alleged links with Russia and his administration's security leaks.

27 May 2017
Ingram Pinn
Financial Times

27 May 2017
Ben Jennings

i

Theresa May's poll lead plummeted following a series of Tory gaffes and an unexpectedly popular Labour manifesto. According to the cartoonist, 'Theresa May called an election at a time when she thought the opportunity was ripe to crush her opponents (a.k.a. "The Saboteurs") with ease, with the Labour Party looking in disarray with internal conflicts. She then proceeded to think that due to her being in such a good position, she would be able to breeze it without doing anything other than uttering a certain catchphrase (I'm not going to say it!) and certainly without having to meet people or debate the opposition. As we know, this didn't go according to plan.'

Jeremy Corbyn caused controversy by linking terrorist attacks in Britain to the UK government's foreign policy. A lifelong pacifist, Corbyn said that 'many experts . . . have pointed to the connections between wars our government has supported or fought in other countries and terrorism here at home.' Conservatives attacked Corbyn for the comments, alleging that he had previously met with members of the IRA, Hamas and Hezbollah.

28 May 2017
Scott Clissold
Sunday Express

According to the cartoonist, 'Theresa May sent the home secretary, Amber Rudd, to stand in for her at the BBC election debate, for which she was roundly criticised. Attempting to defend police cutbacks, reductions in disability payments and the rise of food banks, Rudd had been hung out to dry by the prime minister. Throughout the campaign, May constantly evaded the public and journalists. Ducking the debate symbolised her disdain for democratic engagement but also the unravelling of a campaign that had focused on May's personality.'

2 June 2017
Seamus Jennings
Daily Telegraph

Donald Trump pulled America out of the Paris climate accords, the 2015 agreement that aimed to limit global warming. Theresa May soon came under fire for refusing to condemn the US president's decision. According to Ben Jennings, 'Fellow cartoonist Martin Rowson and I had previously joked that Trump may be purposely trying to exacerbate global warning to melt away all the "special snowflakes". I wouldn't put it past him . . .'

3 June 2017
Ben Jennings
i

5 June 2017
Christian Adams
London Evening Standard

A terrorist attack in London left 11 people dead. Three men drove a white van into pedestrians on London Bridge, then got out and ran through pubs and bars in Borough Market stabbing bystanders. The mayor, Sadiq Khan, described the attack as 'deliberate and cowardly', saying Londoners would not be cowed by terrorism.

Having been suspended in the wake of the London Bridge terrorist attack, general election campaigning resumed on 5 June. Policing now became the focus of debate: Jeremy Corbyn criticised Theresa May for presiding over cuts to police budgets when she was home secretary, and the prime minister accused Labour of undermining the police by opposing giving them greater anti-terror powers.

6 June 2017
Morten Morland
The Times

7 June 2017
Peter Brookes
The Times

Donald Trump attacked Mayor of London Sadiq Khan on Twitter for his response to the London terror attacks. Trump tweeted, 'At least 7 dead and 48 wounded in terror attack and Mayor of London says there is "no reason to be alarmed!"' Khan hit back at the president in a statement, explaining that his comments had referred specifically to the increased police numbers in the capital.

Ex-FBI chief James Comey criticised Donald Trump at a Congress committee hearing. Comey said that Trump had told 'lies, plain and simple' in an attempt to undermine the FBI's probe into the White House's alleged links with Russia. It was the second major political intervention by Comey: in October 2016, at a crucial moment in the presidential election campaign, he had reopened an investigation into Democratic Nominee Hillary Clinton's alleged misuse of a private email server, sparking criticism that he would influence voters.

9 June 2017
Patrick Blower
Daily Telegraph

9 June 2017
Christian Adams
London Evening Standard

Having spent the election campaign promising 'strong and stable government', Theresa May lost the Conservative Party's parliamentary majority, leaving the country with a hung Parliament. Facing calls for her resignation, the prime minister confirmed that she would attempt to form a new government in order to 'provide certainty' for the British people.

Theresa May's Brexit strategy – based on her famously enigmatic statement that 'Brexit means Brexit – was thrown into disarray by the Tories' disastrous election result. Commentators suggested that, having lost her majority, May would be unable to implement her plan for a 'hard Brexit' that involved leaving the European Single Market. European Commissioner Günther Oettinger reportedly saw the election result as a sign that the British electorate had rejected May's approach to exiting the EU.

11 June 2017
Chris Riddell
Observer

Arlene Foster, leader of the Northern Irish Democratic Unionist Party, was labelled a 'king-maker', as it became apparent that Theresa May's government could only govern with the backing of her MPs. But the prime minister came under fire from moderate Tories like Ruth Davidson because of the DUP's links with right-wing unionist groups such as the Orange Order. The drawn-out negotiations risked causing a postponement of the Queen's Speech—not least because of the amount of time required to inscribe it onto the traditional material, vellum. According to the cartoonist, 'The torrid love affair between the DUP and the Tories, plus the temperamental nature of goatskin, caused a delay to the Queen's Speech.'

13 June 2017
Ian Knox
Belfast Telegraph

PLAYING WITH FIRE...

A devastating fire at Grenfell Tower in Kensington, London, killed dozens of people. The 24-storey tower went up in flames after a fridge-freezer malfunctioned on the fourth floor. In the days that followed, speculation grew that the council block was dangerously flammable because of its poor-quality exterior cladding, leading to fears that other buildings were at risk.

15 June 2017
Peter Brookes
The Times

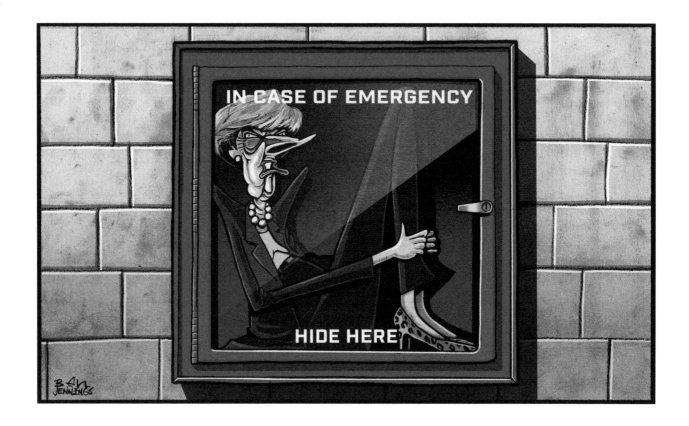

17 June 2017
Ben Jennings
i

Theresa May's poll lead collapsed in the wake of the Grenfell Tower tragedy. According to the cartoonist, 'One thing that seemed to damage Theresa May's credibility throughout the election was her refusal to appear in public. So it was an incredibly bad look when she returned as PM by the skin of her teeth, weakened, and didn't meet residents of the horrific Grenfell Tower fire, citing security concerns (concerns that didn't seem to faze the Queen). It was becoming clearer and clearer that this prime minister wanted to keep her subjects at arm's length.'

A terrorist drove a white van into a group of worshippers leaving Finsbury Park Mosque, shouting, 'I want to kill all Muslims.' This cartoon refers to a photo that circulated on social media showing the van lying abandoned in the street after the attack. The *Daily Mail* responded furiously to Martin Rowson's suggestion that its editorial stance could be linked with the incident. An article entitled 'Fake news, the fascist Left and the REAL purveyors of hatred' said, 'This week the *Guardian* published a cartoon so sick and disgusting – so deranged and offensive to the 4 million decent, humane and responsible people who read us – that we owe it to every one of them to lay to rest this malicious smear.'

20 June 2017
Martin Rowson
Guardian

26 June 2017
David Simonds
London Evening Standard

Jeremy Corbyn appeared on the main stage at Glastonbury Festival, promising that 'the politics that [the general election] got out of the box is not going back in'. According to the cartoonist, 'Jeremy Corbyn wowed the crowds at Glastonbury this year but his stance on Brexit has been very ambiguous, reflecting the divisions between Labour's Remain and Leave supporters.'

In order to secure a working majority in Parliament, the government struck a deal with Northern Ireland's Democratic Unionist Party. Arlene Foster promised that her party's 12 MPs would support Theresa May's legislative agenda; in return, May agreed to £1 billion of investment in the Northern Irish economy.

27 June 2017
Dave Brown
Independent

29 June 2017
Steve Bell
Guardian

The government came under fire for its 'U-turn on a U-turn' over a proposed public sector pay cap. Number 10 hinted that was abandoning the 1 per cent cap on public sector pay rises, before insisting hours later that the policy remained in place. Commentators speculated that the confusion arose from tensions between Theresa May and the chancellor, Philip Hammond, about her economic policy.

Donald Trump responded to Kim Jong-un's latest ballistic missile test by suggesting the Chinese premier, Xi Jinping, could intervene. 'North Korea just launched another missile. Does this guy have anything better to do with his life?' he tweeted. 'Perhaps China will put a heavy move on North Korea and end this nonsense once and for all!'

5 July 2017
KAL
Economist

7 July 2017
Ben Jennings
Guardian

Having said in an interview that she was trying to 'stay out of politics', Donald Trump's daughter Ivanka came under fire for sitting in for the president at a diplomatic summit in Hamburg. The move led to allegations that Ivanka's fashion and perfume business was being treated with nepotism by the Oval Office.

In his first public comments since chairing the Iraq Inquiry, Sir John Chilcot said that former prime minister Tony Blair had not been 'straight with the nation' in the run-up to the Iraq War. Chilcot's comments coincidentally echoed one of Blair's most famous quotes: 'I think most people who have dealt with me think I am a pretty straight sort of guy.' Blair used the original line in 1997, when his government was under fire for exempting Formula One racing from new restrictions on tobacco advertising. It was subsequently invoked by the media every time a scandal rocked Blair's career – from American troops' alleged war crimes in Fallujah to his lucrative advisory role at JP Morgan.

7 July 2017
Steve Bell
Guardian

7 July 2017
Christian Adams
London Evening Standard

Theresa May denied she was a 'lame duck' prime minister as she attended the G20 meeting in Hamburg, her first major summit since the Conservatives' disastrous general election result. In the published version of the cartoon, the wheelchair icon above the words 'Lame Duck Access' was removed because it was deemed in poor taste. Nonetheless, the cartoon faced a backlash on Twitter. One user wrote, 'OK, so it's 2017 but apparently this needs saying: it is NOT OK to compare being politically embattled to being physically disabled. Shame.'

Theresa May said that the supposed risk of vandalism was no reason to give up on proposals to erect a statue of Margaret Thatcher outside Parliament. Meanwhile, there was turmoil in the cabinet as figures including Boris Johnson and Philip Hammond allegedly plotted against May. According to the cartoonist, 'The speech bubble originally read "... would seek to *deface* a great female prime minister" but the editor pointed out that you can't deface a person. It was a bit of a "Yes, that's the joke" situation, but we settled with "trash".'

8 July 2017
Bob Moran
Daily Telegraph

Speaking at the G20 summit in Hamburg, Donald Trump said that a UK–US trade deal would happen 'very quickly'. Theresa May said that she had spoken with the US president and several other leaders who had all expressed a 'strong desire' to create new trade links. However, the prime minister pointed out that the UK was unable to negotiate new trading arrangements with Trump or other leaders such as Angela Merkel and François Hollande until the UK had left the EU.

9 July 2017
Scott Clissold
Sunday Express

Donald Trump defended his son, Donald Trump Jr., who it emerged had met with a Russian lawyer during the presidential election. The president's critics alleged that his campaign staff had taken information about the Democrats from agents of Vladimir Putin. According to the cartoonist, 'This cartoon is about another layer of collusion and electoral interference being revealed, with Donald Trump Jr. admitting he had met with a "Russian lawyer" who was proffering dirt on Hillary.'

13 July 2017
Steven Camley
Scottish Herald

FALLING APART... THE GREAT RE-PEEL

14 July 2017
Dave Brown
Independent

A senior civil servant said that Brexit could make Theresa May's government fall apart 'like a chocolate orange'. Sir Amyas Morse, head of the National Audit Office, warned that different government departments were failing to work together, raising questions about whether Downing Street had a coherent strategy for exiting the EU. Morse's comments came just before the government published its so-called 'Great Repeal Bill', the piece of legislation that allowed Parliament to amend or revoke EU law.

Theresa May asked Jeremy Corbyn for his support in delivering Brexit. The move came as May was facing down dissent from within her own cabinet, with Michael Gove allegedly leaking negative stories about her to the press. According to the cartoonist, 'It amused me that after months of slinging brickbats, slurs and insults at Corbyn, May felt that it was okay to ask for his support over Brexit. Talk about cheek. There was a lot of discussion of the new *Star Wars* film at the time and this classic scene from the original just seemed like a natural fit for the cartoon. Speaking of good fits, doesn't little Michael Gove fit right into the role of Yoda?'

14 July 2017
Rob Moran
Tribune

20 July 2017
Christian Adams
London Evening Standard

Theresa May took a three-week walking holiday in the Swiss and Italian Alps. The prime minister's opponents criticised her decision not to appoint a deputy to cover for her, even though it was a crucial moment in the Brexit negotiations. In the version of this cartoon published in the *London Evening Standard*, the word 'I'm' was omitted for fear that mental health campaigners would think it in bad taste.

The BBC was accused of discrimination after it emerged that most of its highest-paid presenters were men. Two-thirds of the people on its list of top earners were male, with Gary Lineker, Graham Norton and Chris Evans all being paid more than £800,000 per year. Most female stars, such as the *Antiques Roadshow*'s Fiona Bruce, were paid a fraction of that amount.

20 July 2017
Peter Brookes
The Times

Sean Spicer resigned as the White House press secretary. He had become known for his aggressive defences of Donald Trump, often invoking dubious 'alternative facts' to rebut claims made by the media. But he fell from favour after the appointment of Anthony 'the Mooch' Scaramucci as White House communications director. 'Sometimes, you just can't wait for the professional opportunity to draw certain characters,' says the cartoonist. 'Whatever you think of Trump and his ever-changing entourage, they are gifts to the likes of us. Sean Spicer was a particular delight. My great disappointment that his tenure came to an abrupt end was genuine, but temporary. I guess I'm fickle – we may have lost Spicy, but from that void emerged the Mooch.'

23 July 2017
Steve Bright
Sun

Jeremy Corbyn said that he did not promise to write off all student debt while appealing to young voters during the general election. During the campaign, the Labour leader had said he would 'deal with' graduates burdened with the £9,000 fees introduced in 2012. But when quizzed on the comments, he said that he had never promised to get rid of the entire debt. Many Tory MPs and newspapers said that this was a U-turn and that he had misled students.

24 July 2017
Christian Adams
London Evening Standard

According to the cartoonist, 'The summer holidays kicked off with some of the worst weather since February. In fact, we were told to expect "a family of depressions" over the next few weeks. This seemed too tempting not to use. The parallels with what must have been Theresa May's state of mind were too obvious. She had called an election to shore up her majority and squandered it. Now she was fair game – exposed as brittle, superficial and rudderless after a dreadful election campaign and left with a minority government held together by the dreaded DUP. She had cultivated no friends over the years, so her cabinet began to squabble publicly over the legacy. Hammond staked his claim, while the Three Brexiteers (Fox, Davis and Johnson) briefed and bickered with each other like spoilt children realising mummy wasn't going to be around long.'

25 July 2017
Andy Davey
Daily Telegraph

Environment Secretary Michael Gove clashed with his counterpart at the Department for International Trade, Liam Fox, over food standards after Brexit. Fox had suggested that, after leaving the EU, the UK could import goods from the US that did not adhere to European regulations – such as chicken that had been treated with a chlorine wash. But Gove said that the US would have to 'kiss goodbye' to any deal that required Britain to lower standards. The clash renewed speculation that the cabinet was split over how best to quit the EU.

27 July 2017
Dave Brown
Independent

28 July 2017
Christian Adams
London Evening Standard

The veteran Republican Senator John McCain voted against Donald Trump's healthcare reforms. The bill, which had attempted to repeal Barack Obama's healthcare reforms, fell after critics warned that it would lead over 20 million people to lose their health insurance. The move came only days after Donald Trump had described McCain as a 'brave American hero' for returning to Congress to vote despite having a brain tumour.

The government launched an investigation into the costs and benefits of immigration from the EU. The home secretary, Amber Rudd, commissioned the Migration Advisory Committee to assess the economic and social contributions made by EU nationals as a way to ensure there was no 'cliff edge' for employers after Brexit. But the government came under fire for asking for the report to be published in September 2018, only months before Britain will formally leave the EU in March 2019. The scaffold and nooses were omitted from the published version of this cartoon because they were considered to be in bad taste.

28 July 2017
Steve Bell
Guardian

Donald Trump announced that he intended to ban transgender people from serving in the military. In a series of tweets, the president said, 'Our military must be focused on decisive and overwhelming victory and cannot be burdened with the tremendous medical costs and disruption that transgender [sic] in the military would entail.' The comments angered civil rights campaigners, who had previously condemned Trump for his attitude towards women and minority groups – not least for his infamous brag that he liked to 'grab [women] by the pussy'.

30 July 2017
Will McPhail
Sunday Times

Philip Hammond reportedly told business leaders that the government was hoping to maintain existing trading conditions with Europe until 2021, contradicting the 'hard Brexit' stance of politicians including Liam Fox, David Davis and Boris Johnson. According to the cartoonist, 'This cartoon was about warning the prime minister that while she was enjoying her lengthy Swiss/Italian holiday, "Remainer" Chancellor Philip Hammond was gleefully and wilfully leading his cabinet colleagues into a Brexit trap, prolonging negotiations that might even result in keeping Britain within the EU. Treachery and sabotage afoot . . . !'

31 July 2017
Steve Bright
Sun

Donald Trump fired Anthony Scaramucci only ten days after appointing him as White House communications director. He was forced out following a series of gaffes that culminated in him attacking Trump's chief strategist, Steve Bannon, in a *New Yorker* interview. Scaramucci was the latest in a series of high profile departures from Trump's team – Chief of Staff Reince Priebus and Spokesman Sean Spicer had both left their positions days previously. Dave Brown wasn't the only person to notice the similarity between Scaramucci's name and the famous 'Scaramouch' referred to in Queen's song 'Bohemian Rhapsody': the *Merriam-Webster Dictionary* reported that there was a massive spike in searches for the song's lyrics in late July.

2 August 2017
Dave Brown
Independent

Shadow cabinet members called on senior Labour figures including John McDonnell, Ken Livingstone and Jeremy Corbyn to condemn the president of Venezeula, Nicolás Maduro. Corbyn's critics said that his left-wing views meant he was refusing to criticise the socialist president, even though Venezeula had collapsed into chaos and political violence. Corbyn had previously praised Maduro's regime in June 2015, saying his success in areas like health and education were a 'cause for celebration'.

3 August 2017
Morten Morland
The Times

TEMPERATURES ON THE RISE IN EUROPE...

...CHANGEABLE BACK HOME

No.10

BREXIT

Brian Adcock.com 06·08·17

A heatwave in southern Europe resulted in some of the warmest August days on record. In Britain, where temperatures were more reasonable, rumours continued to spread that cabinet members including David Davis, Boris Johnson and Philip Hammond were scheming to replace Theresa May as prime minister – despite the fact that negotiations with Angela Merkel and other EU leaders were still ongoing. According to the cartoonist, 'A slow news day meant having to use the old trick of combining news stories to get a gag. What I really liked about doing this one was, because of the relative simplicity of the cartoon composition, it meant I had more time to exaggerate and get as much expression in their faces as possible. What a wonderfully gruesome bunch.'

6 August 2017
Brian Adcock
Independent

The United Nations Security Council approved new sanctions against North Korea, as Kim Jong-un continued to develop his country's nuclear capabilities. Pyongyang had tested two intercontinental missiles in July, claiming that it aimed to drown the US in 'an unimaginable sea of fire'. The new sanctions banned North Korean exports and limited investment in the country.

7 August 2017
Nicola Jennings
Guardian

Justin Gatlin was booed at the World Athletics Championships in London while collecting his 100m gold medal. The controversial sprinter, who has served two bans for doping, unexpectedly beat Christian Coleman and Usain Bolt into second and third places in the final. According to the cartoonist, 'Anyone who knows me will be aware that I have very little interest in sport, so a sports cartoon always presents a particular challenge. Having said that, it can be nice to get away from politics once in a while. Especially during these gloomy times.'

7 August
Peter Schrank
The Times

After Kim Jong-un promised to fire missiles at the US Pacific territory of Guam, Donald Trump threatened North Korea with 'fire and fury like the world has never seen'. The US president later tweeted that 'Military solutions are now fully in place, locked and loaded, should North Korea act unwisely.' Many diplomatic experts criticised Trump's comments, saying they had unnecessarily increased the risk of nuclear war.

10 August 2017
KAL
Economist

Trump came under fire for failing to condemn a right-wing rally in Charlottesville, Virginia, in which white supremacists and the 'alt-right' violently attacked counter-protestors. According to the cartoonist, 'Is Trump a gift to cartoonists? Well, up to a point. Sure, almost every day brings another jaw-dropping outrage, but how many times can you say that he is an appalling human being and beneath contempt? After a while it becomes repetitive to complain about him . . . Also there's the additional problem that it increasingly just isn't funny – as in this instance. Swastikas have been used in cartoons to smear politicians from Richard Nixon to Angela Merkel. Mostly this is grossly unfair and in very bad taste. Sadly, it's entirely justified here.'

14 August 2017
Peter Schrank
The Times

BARCELONA

Fourteen people were killed when a terrorist drove a van into a crowd in Barcelona, Spain. Younes Abouyaaqoub, a member of a large Islamist cell, ploughed into pedestrians on the city's famous boulevard Las Ramblas. This image, which refers to Picasso's masterpiece *Guernica* – itself a depiction of the bombing of that city in 1937 – was one of several cartoon tributes to the victims published the following day.

19 August 2017
Dave Brown
Independent

The veteran TV presenter Bruce Forsyth, known for presenting the family quiz show *The Generation Game*, died at the age of 89. Meanwhile, Donald Trump fired his chief strategist, Steve Bannon – just weeks after replacing White House staff including Anthony Scaramucci, Sean Spicer and James Comey. According to the cartoonist, 'I thought this was a neat way of acknowledging Bruce Forsyth's death without having to draw the man himself. I'm not sure Americans would understand the reference here at all. Never mind. Cuddly toy!'

20 August 2017
Bob Moran
Daily Telegraph

Donald Trump condemned the removal of statues that celebrated Confederate figures from the American Civil War. His comments came after a series of statues were pulled down by protestors and removed by local governments, following claims that they celebrated racists. 'Sad to see the history and culture of our great country being ripped apart with the removal of our beautiful statues and monuments,' he tweeted. Trump caused further controversy later, saying at a rally of his supporters that, 'With the exception of the late, great, Abraham Lincoln, I can be more presidential than any president that's ever held this office.'

20 August 2017
Morten Morland
Sunday Times

21 August 2017
Ben Jennings
Guardian

Stephen Hawking, the theoretical physicist renowned for his research on black holes, said he was worried about the future of the NHS. He said that the health secretary, Jeremy Hunt, was 'cherry picking' evidence to justify policies that were harming the health service. Hunt hit back at Hawking by saying that the physicist was making claims 'without any evidence at all'.

MPs gathered outside the Houses of Parliament as Big Ben chimed for the last time for four years. The tower fell silent so that workers could undertake restoration work in the tower without damaging their hearing. A number of politicians had unsuccessfully called for the modernising speaker, John Bercow, to intervene to ensure that the bell continued to ring.

22 August 2017
Patrick Blower
Daily Telegraph

23 August 2017
Steve Bell
Guardian

Donald Trump announced that the US would deploy thousands more troops to Afghanistan. During the election campaign Trump had said that his goal was to pull American soldiers out of the troubled region as soon as possible – but in a surprise move, the president said he now thought it was necessary to send 4,000 more soldiers in order to 'push onward to victory'.

As Brexit negotiations continued, Labour accused the government of a U-turn on whether the European Court of Justice (ECJ) would be able to influence UK law after Britain leaves the EU. A new tranche of policy papers suggested that the government intended to allow the ECJ to be involved in adjudicating trade disputes with Europe. Meanwhile, it was announced that partially self-driving lorries would be trialled on British roads by the end of 2018.

26 August 2017
Martin Rowson
Guardian

27 August 2017
Chris Riddell
Observer

David Davis, the secretary of state for leaving the EU, was criticised for lacking a clear Brexit strategy. He clashed with Labour over whether Britain should seek a 'transitional agreement' with the EU in the years immediately after Britain leaves, and was also criticised for his ambiguous policies on migration from the EU and the future role of the European Court of Justice. Davis's opponents had frequently suggested he lacked a plan ever since he was photographed with no notes in front of him on the first day of negotiations with the EU.

According to the cartoonist, 'This cartoon related to the announcement by Shadow Brexit Secretary Keir Starmer and Jeremy Corbyn that Labour's policy on Europe would look considerably more like a 'soft Brexit' than the 'hard' one adopted by the Tories. It promised a long transition period after the official divorce, involving membership of the Customs Union and the Single Market.' The policy aimed to avoid the 'cliff edge' that Theresa May and Boris Johnson had been accused of walking towards. 'To Remainers, the policy seemed like simple common sense, but it was roundly condemned by MPs in vulnerable northern Leave constituencies,' says Davey.

28 August 2017
Andy Davey
Independent

31 August 2017
Patrick Blower
Daily Telegraph

Kezia Dugdale unexpectedly resigned as leader of Scottish Labour. Senior Labour sources told journalists that Dugdale had been 'hounded out by Jeremy Corbyn's mob' and the pro-Corbyn group Momentum, alleging that the Islington MP wanted a more left-wing leader of the party in Scotland. In a statement, Corbyn thanked Dugdale for her 'tireless service', saying he looked forward to working with her to build 'a country that works for the many, not the few'.

Theresa May vowed to stay on as prime minister, telling journalists, 'I am not a quitter.' Speculation had been mounting that Theresa May intended to step down once the government had negotiated a Brexit deal with the EU. But during a visit to Japan, the prime minister said that she intended to fight the next election as leader of the Conservative Party. Meanwhile, Britons commemorated the twentieth anniversary of the death of Princess Diana. After her death, Tony Blair famously described Diana as the 'People's Princess': 'That is how she will stay, how she will remain in our hearts and our memories for ever,' he said.

31 August 2017
Christian Adams
London Evening Standard